YOUR VOICE AND HOW TO USE IT

Cicely Berry

By the same author
VOICE AND THE ACTOR
THE ACTOR AND THE TEXT

This second revised edition published in Great Britain in 2000 by
Virgin Publishing Ltd
Thames Wharf Studios
Rainville Road
London W6 9HA

First revised edition published in 1994
by Virgin Books
a division of Virgin Publishing Ltd

Reprinted 1995

First published in Great Britain 1975
by Harrap Limited

Reprinted 1981, 1982, 1985, 1987, 1990

ISBN 0 86369 826 3

Printed and bound in Great Britain by
Mackays of Chatham PLC, Chatham, Kent

Contents

Diagrams in text

Acknowledgments

We would like to thank the following for their kind permission to print the poems and extracts included in this book:

For 'The Hunchback in the Park' from *Collected Poems* by Dylan Thomas; J. M. Dent & Sons Ltd, the Trustees for the copyrights of the late Dylan Thomas and from *The Poems of Dylan Thomas*. Copyright 1943 by New Directions Publishing Corporation. Reprinted by permission of New Directions Publishing Corporation, New York. For the extracts from *Under Milkwood* by Dylan Thomas; J. M. Dent & Sons Ltd, the Trustees for the copyrights of the late Dylan Thomas and from Dylan Thomas, *Under Milkwood*. Copyright 1954 by New Directions Publishing Corporation. Reprinted by permission of New Directions Publishing Corporation, New York. For an extract from *A Portrait of the Artist as a Young Man* by James Joyce; Jonathan Cape Ltd, the Executors of the James Joyce Estate, The Society of Authors as the literary representative of the Estate of James Joyce, copyright © 1964 by the Estate of James Joyce. All rights reserved. Reprinted by permission of The Viking Press Inc., New York. For 'Foxtrot' from *Facade and Other Poems* by Edith Sitwell; Duckworth, London and David Higham Associates Ltd, London.

Introduction

I am very pleased that Virgin have decided to reissue this book now, in 2000, a quarter of a century after it was written. From a personal point of view, it means that the book is still useful: by giving a certain technical grounding to help people find their own voice, it gives them the confidence to speak in public – and that gives me great pleasure. But, most importantly, this reissue gives us the opportunity to look at the whole process of communicating in public, its value to society, and how our response to it has changed over the last 25 years.

What I find so interesting is that, though we are not a verbal culture as such, people are still drawn by the spoken word; it is innate in all of us – children love being told stories – and I believe we are still drawn by the vibration of the human voice, and still get pleasure from the sound and form of a speech well made. What is more, I believe this to be of vital import to our society at the moment for, in this day of Internet technology, management jargon and minimal communication, our whole way of relating to one another is in the balance: if we are not careful it will be the people who have the right shorthand jargon, and who present facts fast, who will rule, and those with perhaps a fuller and richer understanding of what is going on around them, an understanding of the human condition, who will become the underclass. But I believe this need not come about, for a good speaker can present his/her argument in a way that stimulates both the mind and the imagination of the listener, and can make his/her audience want to discuss, want to talk, want to communicate. This, I believe, is fundamental to the future of our society and of democracy.

I know a great many people worry deeply about how they speak and how they sound, and that this anxiety often stops them expressing themselves as fully as they would wish. The aim of this book, therefore, is to enable you to speak clearly and with confidence in a public situation. When I say 'public' I do not necessarily mean getting up in front of an audience; I mean saying anything in an open or formal situation – perhaps a meeting with colleagues, or between friends coming together to discuss an issue. And I believe this can be done quite simply – through a good understanding of how your voice works, and through quite straightforward and practical exercises.

I think there is little that gives more immediate pleasure than when, while talking with other people, you have a good creative thought and say it at that moment 'just right': it makes you feel quite elated! But at a deeper level, when you have a strong feeling about an issue, be it personal or public, and have managed to express it in exactly the right way, i.e. with shape and precision, this too brings a sense of satisfaction: it has put something in place. If what you were expressing was painful, it may even help to heal. The important thing is that you felt in charge of the situation and of yourself: you were articulate for that moment. Yet how seldom do we feel in charge in this way.

Now when you think how innate language is within us, how much it is part of our everyday life, I want to question why this is so, and why so many people find it extremely difficult, even painful, to express themselves out loud – which is in itself public. The answer is of course complex, because so many things influence how we speak and how the voice reacts to different social situations, so I want to look briefly at what those influences might be and how the exercises can help. There are four main headings:

   i)   the personal (how we arrive at our own voice)
   ii) the social (how we react to other people)
  iii) the public (the different public expectations and modes)
  iv) the practical (the reason for the exercises)

One further thing, but perhaps the most important: you will only feel confident if you feel you are being true to yourself.

First – the *personal* angle/influence.
Your voice is the means by which you convey your inner self and your inner thoughts and feelings in an immediate way to other people – the outside world. It is the outward expression of your inner self, a sort of channel from inside to outside, and is therefore a very particular expression of you and of your personality.

I think we all have what I call a 'secret' voice: a voice that we hear inside our heads, which conveys exactly what we want, how we think and feel, yet that voice so seldom tallies with what in the end comes out. The inner image does not fit with the outer one – or rather the voice that other people hear does not tally with that inner image. Why?

I will try to answer. We arrive at our voice via a very circuitous route: to begin with, it is to do with what you hear when you are a child – in other words, what there is to copy. But this is quite complex, for how you copy what you hear is conditioned by how you relate to those around you, and how you choose to copy it: this is governed by your personality, and is therefore a choice quite early on, albeit an instinctive one. (I will go into this in more detail in the next chapter.) The important thing to realise is that our habits of speech are formed very early and quite unconsciously: they are part of our body growth, as it were, and cannot be changed easily.

But then as we grow older and go to school we become part of a social situation: we start to make our voice behave according to a received idea of how we think we should sound. We start to monitor it, subliminally of course: we start to make it conform – or not conform if we wish to rebel, and that is our choice. None of this is what might be termed 'psychological', but is simply to do with how we unconsciously motivate ourselves in order to survive as well as possible. But our habits stay with us, so if you were told to 'speak up' when you were small – I think one of the worst things that can be said to a child – that may well continue to be said. Sadly the habit will become more deeply rooted, perhaps because you are self-conscious and do not want to be noticed – but all too often some of that feeling remains with us.

For criticism of your voice comes uncomfortably close to being a criticism of you as a person. For instance, if someone asks you to repeat what you have said because they have not heard you properly, being either not clear or not loud enough, you unconsciously resent this as you assume that your voice is inadequate. Or if you are interrupted while telling a story, you assume you are not being sufficiently interesting, and do not want to finish. In both cases, your confidence is undermined.

As you will therefore suspect, a great deal depends on how confident you were made to feel as a child in expressing yourself: this in turn depends on whether your family liked to talk and express their feelings – and this is not strictly to do with class or education, it is to do with the habit, ethos, of each particular family and culture. But of course, ultimately class does play a huge part in self-confidence, and we must be honest about this: the class or culture which surrounds you forms the background within which you can feel at ease. It is much more difficult to feel confident in company if you do not have a certain social experience/background, or, and this is also crucial, if you feel you have missed out on a full education. This has no correlation with how much you have to offer as a person, but it does have a bearing on your ability to act/speak with authority.

Also I think some people are born with quite a natural vocal response – they want to talk: we recognize that some people have what we call 'a musical ear' and have naturally good singing voices, and in the same way I believe some people have a feel for words – they like poetry for instance, and this gives them a kind of vocal/verbal confidence from the beginning. It is a gift and we must recognize it as such, but it is also something that we can acquire.

Secondly – the *social* angle.

We carry all this 'voice baggage' with us into the adult world, into our career, business, whatever: we obviously learn a lot on the way and get better at communicating etc., but the background habits and vocal patterns are still with us.

So the next step is to learn how to be objective about your voice: and this is particularly difficult because, as we have seen, we have such a subjective response to it. It is subjective not only because of the habits we have grown up with, and the memories and associations that stick, but also because you hear your own voice via the bone conduction in your own head, and this gives it a different resonance: you are therefore not hearing it as other people do. This accounts for the shock when you hear your recorded voice for the first time: it often seems unrecognizable, and this is not simply because of the recording mechanism, but because you are hearing it via the outside waves and your outer ear. You are hearing it as someone else: and this is where you need to be objective.

Here I want to say two things which may seem contradictory: first I think that in our wish, or rather need, to fit in and to sound intelligent, we become too conditioned by what we think other people expect of us – we make our voice 'behave'. If we are not careful our secret voice gets lost – we stop listening for it. Yet at the same time we have to be realistic: we may have irritating vocal habits of which we are not aware and which may be alienating and give the wrong impression, so we have to be sensible. We have to believe that we are good enough, and that what we have to say is important: we also have to learn to make any necessary adjustments in order that our voice conveys exactly what we intend, and how we perceive ourselves to be. It is a fine balance.

Thirdly – the *public* angle.

I think it is quite difficult to specify exactly what is expected of us now, for fashions of speech change: you have only to listen to a newsreel of ten years ago to realize this – it does not sound quite real any more. And since I wrote this book in 1975 I think there has been a good deal of change: so let us take an objective look at this.

How we communicate with each other on an everyday basis has become minimalist, and much less formal: technology has taken over more and more. We have become a less verbal society, and when it comes to functioning in public we are more interested in the soundbite than in reasoning things out in depth. Billions of dollars are spent each year by corporate companies to make corporate videos in order to sell their products, which is impersonal communication! This means that when we get up to speak formally, we have to make a bigger adjustment: on the one hand we need to seem informal, but at the same time we are aware that we need to grab attention in as colourful a way as possible, for the vernacular slang is rich and vivid. This is in fact 'being formal' but with a different angle – and so the soundbite was formed.

Let me digress a moment and give you an example. For the last 30 years my main work has been with the Royal Shakespeare Company: as Voice Director for the RSC I have seen, or should I say heard, very clearly the change in speech during this time. I know that because of today's mode of casual speech it is very difficult for young actors – and of course I mean actors of either gender – to feel at home with the colourful and emotionally charged world that Shakespeare conjures for us through the language: it is not that they cannot do it, but that they find it difficult to be truthful within themselves, whilst honouring the imagery and rhythm of that text. It is extravagant language – the very opposite of how we communicate now. We have to work at it in a very specific way, for it is essential for the actor to feel truthful: and I have evolved a number of ways to break through that barrier. I say this because I think it might help to clarify what I mean.

Still on this question of fashions in speech, when you hear that newsreel of 20, or even 10, years ago it will sound affected: and this is because we have become used to a much broader range of accent – which is as it should be. The good thing about television – 'that campfire around which our communities gather' as Helena Kennedy so eloquently puts it – is that it has opened our ears to the great variety within the English language itself, and we are no longer bound by the 'upper class' accent. Twenty years ago, people were trained to speak what we call RP (Received Pronunciation) or what used to be known as an Oxford accent. This was considered educated and proper, and certainly in some jobs your chances of promotion would have been limited if you had any trace of a so-called 'vulgar' or 'non-U' accent. Now there is much more diversity of speech sounds and this gives our language so much more colour and (I think) warmth and humanity.

Just five years ago Tom Leonard, the Scottish poet, wrote a great poem called 'The Six o'Clock News', the essence of which was that people did not believe the news if it was read by someone with a Scottish accent. But I think the wind has changed considerably – though not wholly – and in some cases the reverse now holds true. I have heard that in some quarters the prevailing feeling is that someone with a dialect gives the impression that they can be trusted more, and that this can be a useful attribute if you are in marketing – cynical, but true.

Nowadays, if you speak in an accent, unless there is a very good reason to change it I believe you should keep it. An actor, for instance, needs to be able to speak RP – Received Pronunciation – or he/she would be very limited as to the parts that he/she could be cast for, though I firmly believe that RP should be used as an accent and that the native dialect should not be discarded. But unless there is a practical reason such as this, there is no reason to change it. Your speech is what you grew up with and what you feel comfortable with: and moreover, it is emotionally connected with your way of expressing yourself, which in itself is individual. You just need to make sure that it is muscularly firm and clear.

Fourthly – the *practical* exercises.
Having said all this, the interesting thing is that how we deal with our own voice does not change – the equipment (the breathing, relaxation and muscularity that we need practically to work on) is all the same.

I want to quote from Gwynneth Thurburn, who was my teacher: as Principal of the Central School of Speech and Drama for many years, she initiated the main teaching of Voice in this country, and taught many famous actors. What she wrote about the actor and his/her use of voice still applies now: 'Some kind of period style emerges in every decade or so. We tend to think that something New has been found: that we are verging on the 21st century and so on. Actually most of it is as old as the hills, changing and varying with the times, but its roots were probably always the same. Beware of the NEW and the DISCOVERY unless you know what is new and what has been discovered that nobody knew before.' I like that.

The exercises will help us in the following ways:

i. Good deep breathing centres us, enables us to hear our own real voice, and gives it good resonance. If your work is vocally demanding, as for instance it is for the teacher, then breathing exercises are essential to counteract strain. Voice Training should be part of all Teacher Training Colleges and voice strain should be recognized as a hazard of the job: there is both the mental strain of keeping a group of young people interested, and the continuous physical strain on the voice. There are, after all, many good voice teachers who could take on this work. But whatever our job there is always some tension attached, and good breathing makes us calm and, most important, puts us in touch with our own integrity.

ii. An awareness of relaxation gives us confidence: we cannot be completely relaxed always, for there are times when we need tension to hold us together (e.g. when certain strains in our personal life cannot be left at home), but we can gain sufficient physical awareness to release the muscles involved with the breathing and with the neck resonator so that we get the best use and result from our voice, and this of course will help build confidence.

iii. We can practise the muscularity of the lips and tongue, not in order to speak 'better', but rather with the purpose of releasing our thoughts actively and accurately through the language, so the words have authority and life and people listen. Words are our thoughts in action, and we want to make them immediate in that way.

iv. We can acquire an awareness of pitch and volume: so often a voice which is otherwise good to listen to stays on the same pitch and becomes monotonous and in a way lifeless – it does not draw us to listen and in the end is irritating. Or, and this is quite common, the voice is pitched at the same volume, a fraction too loud, and it seems to be talking 'at' and not 'to' us, and we on the receiving end unconsciously back away – in our minds, of course. This is simply due to a lack of objective judgement on the part of the speaker, and can be put right very quickly.

All these things can be worked at, not in order to alter your voice or make it 'marketable' or 'effective' in an untruthful way, but rather so that you get the best use out of it and, most important, that it may reflect what you think and feel as accurately as possible – and as you would wish. But remember that when you do make these adjustments, because you are hearing them inside your head, the difference will seem big to you at first: do not be put off by this, for the exercises will merely get you to use what is natural in order to speak, and they will in fact make you sound more at ease. However, it will take time to believe this – there is always a time-lag between doing and believing! It is good if there is someone you can trust who you can sound out on what is happening.

As far as building a speech is concerned, always remember that people get pleasure out of hearing others speak well: we will deal with this fully in the final chapter. I believe it is useful to practise on good speeches: prop up Shakespeare on your mantelpiece and read it aloud, or find a book of well-known public speeches and do the same with them: feel the shape and the music – it is exciting. As I have already said, we no longer live in a verbal society, in which people sit down and tell stories to each other: instead we sit passively and watch television and listen to other people talk. We need to get people excited by language again. I have done a good deal of work on Shakespeare in prisons, and I have watched how excited a group will get by speaking this physical language, and I am convinced that if we could release people's desire to speak and to release their feelings through words, there would be less violence around us.

Looking again at what has been written in the book, it is interesting to see that the basic means have not changed, for the speaker still needs to work on his/her voice, i.e. to find the relaxation, to discover his/her potential resonance, and to work on the definition of the language. Nor has the basic format of a speech changed: the shaping of a speech is still of the utmost importance, for it still needs those three main elements:

i. opening with a provocative statement or question in order to state the premise

ii. the building up of the argument: three or four main ideas – ideally with some alliteration

iii. the winding up, the ending – perhaps leaving us with a question, something unanswered to hover in our minds

These points are analyzed fully in *Our Masters' Voices*, a very interesting book by Max Atkinson which is well worth reading. There is something dynamic in that format which appeals to all, and makes us want to hear more, but you have to play around with the form for yourself and make it your own to see if it works for you. And, very importantly, always leave a split moment between thoughts to allow time for each idea to drop for the listener – and to make him/her hungry for more.

By working at all this, we can get the best possible use from our voices – and in the process be as truthful and as accurate as possible in conveying our thoughts and feelings. This is not only helpful and useful, but also makes us more at ease with ourselves – and this is surely worth working for.

And this is something we, those of us who speak in public, also have to work at, for I believe there is something innate in all of us that responds to the rhythm and cadence of a good speech – it has developed over time with our need to express ourselves, our feelings, and connect with the person we are talking to – and we must keep this need alive. Words have the power to excite, provoke, disturb and give pleasure. I believe it is our job to excite people with language and make them want to talk.

I think it is very useful that we have the views of speakers from the past as well as the present in this book, for all the speakers who are quoted have that desire to reach an audience, that commitment, that pleasure and that generosity. They all convey their real sense of joy in communicating with others, and there is much we can learn from them. One last point: at the time of writing I chose to use *he* rather than *he/she*, believing it to be less cumbersome. I now regret this, and I apologise to those whose feelings may be offended.

Cicely Berry
January 2000

1

Becoming Aware of Your Voice

1   How vocal sound is made.

Let us see first of all how sound is made. To make any sound at all
two factors are needed — something that strikes and an object that is
struck and which resists the impact to a greater or lesser degree and
vibrates accordingly. These vibrations then disturb the surrounding
air and set up sound waves which you receive through the mechanism
of the ear, which, by a very intricate procedure, sends impulses to
the brain and the result is that you hear a sound. All sounds have
these two factors, and their volume will depend on two things — the
hardness of the object struck, and its sensitivity to vibrations — so
that the noise made by walking on a wooden platform will be greater
than the impact of the same footsteps on a stone pavement, for wood
is more pliant than stone and so capable of larger vibrations. It is
the size of the vibrations that determines the volume — of course,
the object that strikes can vibrate too. The more musical the
sound the more regular the vibrations themselves will be, although
we are not aware of this. A musical sound also has a third factor
which helps to give a pattern to the vibrations, and that is a resonator — i.e., something which amplifies the initial sound by setting
up sympathetic vibrations, and amplifying and sustaining that
initial sound sufficiently to allow us to hear a note of a certain
pitch. The resonating factor may be quite crude, as in a zither for
instance, where the strings are simply attached to a piece of wood
of a certain shape and size, and where vibrations respond to the
initial sound set up by the strings. Or the resonator may be a more
elaborate affair like the case of a violin, which has a very particular
shape and size, the resonating vibrations of which give us the particular quality of the violin and make it recognizable as such as opposed
to any other instrument. The resonator contributes its own quality
to the original sound because of the harmonic vibrations it sets up,
and because it sustains that sound so that we hear a distinguishable
note. In fact, in an organ it is the resonant pitch of the pipes that
dominates the initial vibrations made by the reed. Thus it is the
resonator which determines the quality of sound and makes it
particular.

The space in which a sound is made can add its own resonance and alter the quality of the sound. For instance, an empty room will amplify sound more than a furnished one, for material stops vibration and so deadens the sound. Consequently, a stone building, such as a church, with non-porous walls, will bounce sound back off the walls, making even more resonance, and creating its own particular acoustic problems. On the other hand, when sound is made in the open air, the sound waves disperse more quickly as there is no space to contain them, which is why it is always a much greater strain to speak outside as you have little means of judging how far the sound is carrying.

Now let us be specific about how we make our own vocal sound, and for this purpose we will take the violin as an example, because it offers a good analogy with the voice. In a violin the bow strikes the strings causing them to vibrate and thus set up sound waves. This initial note, which is small, is then amplified by the wooden box underneath setting up its own vibrations. The pitch of the note is determined by the tautness and length of the vibrating portion of the string which the player controls with his fingers — the higher the note the shorter the vibrating portion and *vice versa,* and the particular size and shape of the violin box sets up its own vibrations, which are the harmonics of the original note, and gives them the particular quality which we recognize as belonging to a violin. However, the quality of sound can vary enormously between one violin and another, because of the difference of materials used, the precise measurements, the particular craftsmanship and so on — all these things determine the precise quality of the individual violin. The sound will also vary because of the way it is played — how the bow actually strikes the strings, etc. — all these factors will make the resonating vibrations or harmonics slightly different. In other words — i) the quality of sound will vary from one violin to another, and ii) the quality from the same violin will vary according to how it is played.

Let us see how this compares with the voice. In the voice the breath acts as the bow which, on exhaling, strikes the vocal cords in the larynx which come together when you want to make sound, and causes them to vibrate. These vibrations set up sound waves which can then be resonated in the chest, the pharynx or hollow space above the larynx, in the mouth, nose and bones of the face and skull, and the hollow spaces in some of the bones of the head — the sinuses. You will see immediately that, although the way in which we make sound is the same, the individual quality of the voice will vary according to the infinite variations in the size and shape of people, and thus the individual voice becomes as distinctive and particular to each person as fingerprints. Just as a good violinist can get sounds out of a violin that a bad player cannot, so, as individuals, we can make good or bad use of the mechanism we have. For instance, the way we use the breath to strike the cords — as the violinist uses his bow — can make the difference to the sound being breathy or glottal or harsh — in fact you can actually damage the voice by striking the cords too harshly with the breath. I said this initial sound can be resonated in the cavities of the chest, neck, mouth, nose, etc., but in fact a lot of people, because of tension and not knowing how to place sound, do not use these resonating cavities to the full, and in a lot of cases hardly use them at all. Now to use these spaces fully does not make the sound over-consciously 'produced' as it were and perhaps similar to other trained voices — as quite rightly you may fear — if properly used it makes the voice more intrinsically your own, for all you are doing is using your own physical structure. But the human voice has another factor which the violin does not have and that is the mobility of the resonators of the mouth, etc. — it can change its size and shape with the movement of the jaw, tongue and palate, so that we can produce variations on the resonance and make words.

Because of the difference in the physical make-up of the individual some people will obviously be able to get more sound than others and anyway some people have naturally more musical voices, but what matters is that you know how to use the breath and the resonating spaces and that you use them as well as possible.

2   *How the individual voice evolves.*

I think it is important to see just how complex an affair it is for the individual to arrive at his own particular voice. As I see it, it is an intricate mixture of four conditioning factors:

  i)   what you hear
 ii)   how you hear it
iii)   the physical make-up of a person and the agility of the muscles involved in making speech
iv)   how you unconsciously choose to use your voice in the light of your personality and experience

   I will take each point separately:

   i) What you hear — by this I mean your environment.
The voice is incredibly sensitive to what is going on around it, and adjusts quickly. In broad terms, the speech of people who live in country districts is quieter, slower and more musical than the speech patterns evolved in cities which are nearly always sharp, glottal and

quick — for example, New York, Glasgow and London, though the accents are different, have similar speech characteristics, because over a period of time voices have adjusted to the noise and pace of those cities and quick glottal speech cuts through noise more efficiently, as well as keeping up with the pace of living. In the same way, but to an infinitely more subtle degree, your voice is conditioned by your family, or the unit in which you grew up. Really, your style of speech and the way you use your voice is set at a very early age and as we grow older we either concur with it and so let it become set, or to some degree rebel against it and so change.

Obviously we learn by listening and imitating. Quite instinctively we convey needs and emotions through sound — we cry or gurgle depending on whether we are hungry or not, loved or not. As our needs and mental faculties become more precise we start to shape these sounds into words and so be particular. This is when the sophistication begins. Words are probably the most sophisticated things we have to deal with — slang being the most sophisticated kind of speech-shorthand of all. But in the mean time all we can do is imitate, and so we imitate those who are nearest.

You learn to speak unconsciously as a child through imitation, so that to begin with you have roughly the same accent and inflection pattern as your parents and you pick up their vocabulary. When you go to school this changes, for you begin to be influenced by people outside the family, and the vocabulary widens. Also, you probably begin to make a difference between the way you speak to grown-ups and how you speak with friends — children are often bi-lingual in this way, for the kind of language and slang used with friends is not always acceptable to teachers and parents. Early on you begin to be aware of other people's reactions to how you speak — i.e., what pleases and what does not — and you adjust accordingly — all through life we unconsciously adjust our speech according to the people we are with. But also, at an early age, your relationships with your family and their reactions to you help to form the way you speak — i.e., whether you expect approval or disapproval, interest or lack of it, refusal or acceptance, patience or impatience. For if you are assured of their sympathy and tolerance, you will at once start off with more confidence in your speech than a child whose parents do not bother to listen. Taking time to listen to a child is perhaps the most valuable key to giving him confidence in later life, and, conversely, telling him to 'shut up' is the most destructive, because it does not merely make him stop talking there and then, it closes up his desire to express his feelings and so begins to close up his personality. Early responses help to set the tone and inflection pattern; if you can expect interest, your voice will be more positive and resolved in inflection, whereas if the expectation is of refusal and lack of interest, you will adopt a high-pitched whining tone, because it is more penetrating and is actually physically irritating to the ear and so demands attention. This results later in minor tone, unresolved inflections and aggrieved sound. Obviously these are very general indications — because all children 'grizzle' at times anyway — and all these things modify as you grow up, but certainly the general atmosphere is formative. I was working with an actor recently who has had quite a lot of experience in the theatre and has done a good deal of voice work. One day he told me that in order to do voice exercises and make loud sounds he had consciously to tell himself that it was all right for him to do so. He had grown up in an atmosphere where you had to be quiet, where his mother was constantly nagging at quite ordinary justifiable noise so that in the end he whispered, and he still had a strong sense of guilt when he spoke loudly. When he told me that, it made absolute sense because I had always felt he was holding his voice back, and that the tensions he had were caused by inhibiting the natural power of his voice so that it sounded over-controlled.

Also, of course, how much you talk as a family is important, for some families are much freer with each other than others — how articulate you are (and by this I do not mean educated) what position in the family you are, whether it is quiet or noisy, and to what extent you accept or reject them. If it is noisy and loud, you may do the reverse of this and mumble. If you resent a strong or 'common' accent, you may go for more standard speech — or if the family speech is upper-class you may go against this and try to sound working-class. All sorts of permutations arise.

So you see, it is not only what you hear around you in your environment that helps to form your voice and speech, but also your attitude to that environment. You will add your own particular experience to this — but it is all part of how you arrive at your voice.

ii) How you hear — by this I mean how accurately you perceive
     the sound you hear — and this we will call 'ear'.
Some people perceive sounds and rhythms more accurately and distinctly than others, and are more aware of their qualities and more able to reproduce them accurately. Just as some people have a better musical 'ear' than others, so people's ear for speech varies, though, curiously, a good ear for music and a good ear for speech do not necessarily go together — often the reverse in fact.

Some people, quite early on, have preferences and make choices with regard to the speech they use — that is to say that someone with a strong regional accent listens to announcers on radio or television, is influenced by them and chooses to adjust his speech accordingly — this can make him bi-lingual in the reverse way to that mentioned earlier — i.e., he uses his regional accent at home and a more standard conformist accent outside at work or with friends. He becomes conscious of a wider spectrum of speech sounds and because he has a responsive ear easily makes the physical adjustments. This also has something to do with a lack of inhibition in making different sounds and perhaps a need to fit in with the people around him. Another person may have the facility to do this but choose not to — for some people it is embarrassing to alter anything about their speech. It is interesting to note that it is always inhibiting to be told you are not singing in tune — it actually stops you from being able to hear properly.

Certainly your ear conditions how you interpret what you hear, and so how you speak. Also, of course, there are many people who find real pleasure in words, they enjoy listening to people speak well, they enjoy using words themselves and relish them, not only for their logical meaning but on other levels — e.g., the sound they make and the physical making of them, their sound associations, and associations of meaning. This is a gift that some people have to a highly developed degree — quite a lot of people, in fact, when you think of the numbers who enjoy poetry recitals and festivals, and take part in them, or who read poetry aloud to themselves. Others enjoy good oratory and are very aware of the emotive value of speech rhythms — you have only to read any of Churchill's speeches, for instance, to be aware of their rhythmic power and the very basic primitive responses we have to that kind of speaking. This enjoyment is much more a part of us than we think, for we must not forget that forms of words played a vital part in primitive religions, in prayer chants and incantations to keep away evil spirits, etc., and that the forms of these words themselves had a special power. This emotive power from language rhythms is still a part of us and we are moved by it — it still remains in the liturgies of the church, in some poetry and oratory, and is distinct from words used in the normal everyday way to communicate thoughts and needs. To many people good language is an exciting and enriching experience, for words take on a physical life of their own and resonances of meaning beyond logical sense. This is also true of good comedy and witty comedians — we delight in the play of words and in a comedian who can 'do' things with words, giving them all sorts of meaning apart from the purely logical. Children, I think, find great pleasure in word rhythms — you have only to listen to chants they make up to skipping games to realize this — playgrounds are a rich source of word and rhythm patterns.

Pleasure in sound can play an important part in forming your speech habits, and it is something which, unfortunately, we do not develop enough in children. This pleasure is particularly true of people whose native speech was originally some form of Gaelic — the race memory is there even though they may not speak the language. The Irish delight in being verbal, and even their everyday expressions have a poetic turn and cadence beyond that of an English person's experience. Welsh people delight in the musicality of language — the Welsh language itself is highly developed musically and vowel sounds will be changed, not because of sense, but according to their musical position in a phrase. However, that is part of a different language tradition. Some people do not find this pleasure in verbal sound and even distrust it, and so they perhaps find it more difficult to commit themselves verbally — I think this is very much an English trait. It can result in the voice being restricted in range, and perhaps dull — but of course the individual personality has much to do with it.

The point is, the more developed your ear is, the more open you are to the possibilities of what your voice can do, and so the more interesting it can be. And it can be developed by listening to what you hear around you and by reading different styles of text aloud and discovering for yourself the possibilities of rhythm, texture and cadence in the language. Often the most difficult part is to break through the barrier of your own inhibition, for at first when you hear your voice expanding and using notes that you have not used before you feel slightly false, for it does not sound like you — but that is a matter of your own ear adjusting to it. To other people you may not sound false — simply more interesting. Through a process of exercises you will come to be able to judge for yourself.

iii) The physical make-up of a person, and the agility of the
    muscles involved in making speech — the physiological resources.
It is obvious that the physical size and shape of a person help to determine the vocal quality. A largely-built person has a potentially larger chest capacity for breath, so the volume could be greater. Also a large chest and neck has more resonating value and should make the sound fuller. This is easy to understand, but it does not always work like this — for we all know quite large people with small voices, and small people with a lot of range, power and resonance. Therefore it is how you use your physical resources that counts — i.e., your breath and the resonating spaces of the chest and neck. In other words — the muscular firmness with which you can respond to the sound heard in the head. Some people are lucky and use these resources naturally and this has a lot to do with what we have

already talked about — how you were brought up to speak and how you expect to sound — but it also has to do with how relaxed and solid you are as a person — the more relaxed you are the more deeply you are likely to breathe so that your voice will be rooted and the resonating spaces will be fully used. Someone who does a lot of physical training will probably develop his breathing capacity more than a less active person, but he will not necessarily be relaxed and he will not necessarily breathe deeply.

So, some people use their potential resonance more than others, but this is something you can deal with because all these physical resources can be developed.

It is the same with speech — it is the degree of muscular agility in the muscles that move the jaw, tongue, lips and palate that determines the clarity of your speech. And, unless there is any physical difficulty — such as an extra-large tongue, which can be difficult to manage, or a short frenum, which is the string-like ligament underneath your tongue, which would make the tongue difficult to stretch — or any other such impediment, there is no reason why everyone should not have the clarity of speech they require.

Lack of clarity in speech is partly to do with habit — i.e., patterns already set up in childhood, which incidentally has nothing to do with laziness, as is so often thought — but partly also to do with your commitment to speaking. And this of course is involved with whether you are shy or not, introverted or not, etc., and to some extent is conditioned by education and the kind of vocabulary you have and your confidence in using it. But it also has much to do with your need to communicate. For instance, dancers often have poor voices because they give expression to their feelings through another medium — writers and painters are often curiously hesitant in their speech. And someone whose job is carried out for the most part alone, or which requires analytical thought, so that his energy is contained within himself, very often finds it quite difficult to be verbal. It is interesting to notice that if you have been alone for a period of time — a day or two — it takes quite a bit of mental effort to speak again because you have become withdrawn. For someone who has been in prison for a lengthy period this kind of verbal withdrawal must be an enormous barrier — something which would take time and help to overcome.

I remember once teaching a research chemist who was brilliant and whose main work was in research at a university. However, he also had to lecture, and he came to me for advice because he could not be understood beyond the first few rows. In fact he was almost unintelligible, for the muscles which move the lips, tongue and palate were so slack that the consonants — the sounds that make the words

20

carry — hardly existed. In conversation he could be understood, but as soon as he spoke louder in order to reach more people, the consonants just did not balance the increased volume so that you only heard the vowels — i.e., the middle of the words — and not the beginnings and ends; it was so bad it was an impediment. As I got to know him better I was convinced it was because, even as a child, he was so engrossed in his own thoughts and, probably, left alone with them — he preferred reading to talking — that he had never developed a normal facility to make words. It was as simple as that. By very straightforward muscular exercises in a relaxed state, he gradually became aware of the amount of physical activity required in making clear speech. Obviously to begin with he felt he was exaggerating, but with time he realised the discrepancy between what he thought was clear and what was actually clear to the listener. This is an extreme example, but a good one to make you realise just how interdependent the mental and physical attitude to speech is. For, lack of clarity can also come from not being definite in thought, or from thinking more quickly than you can speak, so that the words are gabbled and the speech is cluttered. The mental intention has to be related to the physical action.

The good thing to remember is that vocal sound and speech is the result of physical action which, by exercise, you can develop and improve.

iv) Personality — character

The voice is conditioned by all these three factors and also by education — not necessarily formal, for some who have gone to the best schools are unbelievably limited in vocabulary, and others with sparse education are very articulate — and by what is expected of us, but in the end it is in the light of our own character and personality that the mixture comes together. For though you start by imitation of whatever attracts that is around you, even at the start you are making the choice between what you choose to imitate and what you choose to discard — in other words you imitate the people you like. And it is your emotional and temperamental reactions to your environment, your degree of sensitivity to other people, your own emotional need to communicate, and your ease or unease in doing so, it is all these things that actually bring the voice together and form the end product.

As you see, the voice is an intricate and interesting mixture. A voice tells us a lot about a person — whether introvert or extrovert, generous or shut in, sympathetic or uninvolved, emotionally closed or open — the voice is the message (to twist McCluhan). However, we must not necessarily take the surface message, for the person who sounds very sympathetic may be covering underlying resentment, and the person who sounds uncaring may be doing so because he is afraid of being hurt. The person who sounds aggressive is likely to be quite timid underneath — you just have to listen. All of these four factors we have talked about are interrelated. I think when you start viewing the voice in this way the barriers you may have about your own voice begin to drop away.

And this brings us to the point where we should examine the image we present.

3   Your vocal image.

The image you have of your own voice is often quite different from the way it sounds to others. You have only to think of people's reactions to hearing themselves on a tape recorder for the first time, to realize this. Most people are surprised and even horrified to find that their voice does not sound in the least as they had imagined. It seems to sound higher in pitch and thinner in quality, often there are mannerisms which are totally unexpected — you speak faster or slower than you think, you sound affected and over-precise, or sloppy with unfinished consonants, or indecisive, you may have a heavier accent than you thought, or, worst of all, you may sound just plain flat and dull, which is very damaging to one's ego!

However, hearing yourself on a tape recorder does not necessarily give a whole impression of your voice, for the machine is more sensitive to some frequencies than to others and so is selective, (a woman's voice frequently comes out sounding higher than it actually is) just as a photograph, though accurate to what it sees, does not give a complete picture of a person — and some people photograph better than others anyway! For you are hearing your voice impersonally, via a machine and without the impressions you communicate through your eyes, face and body — all of which influence how we hear a person and tell us something. (It is interesting to think of the images we create of people we hear on the radio and do not see.) A recording is not a totally accurate representation, though you can learn much from it — about your diction — i.e., what the vowels and consonants sound like — about the amount of inflection you use, about pace — whether you are slow or quick, and whether you vary timing — and above all it trains the ear so that you begin to recognize the areas where how you think you sound does not tally with what you hear on the tape. This is the important use of the tape recorder, but you should never think of it as replacing exercises which have to be done, or as any form of short cut, nor should you use it too much, so that you start listening to your own voice in the wrong kind of way.

The tape recorder is not the only means you have of finding out that you may not sound to others as you think you do. Odd comments people make about how you sound reinforce this and make you aware of the discrepancies. You can be surprised at being told you sound abrupt, rude, cross, aggressive or over-emphatic, when in fact you do not feel any of those things. Or you can give the impression of being disinterested, uncaring and casual when that is not the impression you would want to give, for it is not how you feel. Much of this has to do with how you use your energy — how much energy you put into the vocal sound of the voice and into the making of words. If, on the whole, you give an aggressive impression, then you are over-loading your voice with energy — either with breath so it is too loud, or pressing the consonants out so it is over-emphatic. If you sound disinterested, then you are doing the reverse and not putting enough energy into the sound and the words. Finding your vocal energy and how to place it is probably the most vital thing we shall learn. But at the moment we are concerned with how accurate your voice is being to your intentions, and it is important, from the beginning, to start listening to the behaviour of your own voice and that of other people's — not to listen over-critically or self-consciously, I mean simply to notice what happens. When you are with people with whom you are at ease, notice how easy and relaxed the voice is, and alive, even though you may be talking quietly — remember how this feels. Yet when you are in an unfamiliar situation your voice behaves quite differently — often something false creeps in which you regret — and somehow it does not seem so alive. To develop the voice you have to become aware of it, not by over-indulging in what you think is good sound and listening to yourself in a wrong way, but listening to find out how you are getting across to other people — and that is quite a different matter, for perhaps it will also make you listen to other people more accurately.

Let us see what the reasons are for these differences in the perception of what you hear and what others hear. The simple physical reason is that you hear your own voice via the bone conduction in your head, so the vibrations you hear are different from those heard by other people via outside space — although in certain spaces you get a considerable feedback of your own voice, and if you cup your hands round your ears yet get an approximation of what other people hear. The vibrations in the bones of the head account for the differences in pitch and quality, and lead you to think it is lower and fuller in pitch than it is — and louder, which is why you are surprised (and a little hurt) when you are told you cannot be heard. You often do not quite believe it. How you hear your own sound, and how you learn to be objective about it, varies with your experience. That is why it is so unfair to grumble at children for mumbling, for there is no knowing how they hear themselves, besides which, they are less confident in what they want to express, and have less experience of knowing what can or cannot be heard. So many bad habits are arrived at through insensitive and inaccurate criticism.

The other reason for this discrepancy is far more subtle, for just as you have a private image of yourself — what you look like and how you move — which may not bear much resemblance to what other people see (I know people for instance who are convinced they are clumsy, when in fact that is not the impression they give at all), so you have a private image of your voice which does not necessarily tally with the impression it gives. When you feel sympathetic and interested, by clipped speech and offhand inflections you may sound just the opposite, or you may over-adjust the voice and sound too sympathetic and therefore false. You see, you are on the inside as it were, you know what you are thinking and what you are trying to express, you know how you feel and what your attitude is, and in a way you take for granted that others are tuned in to exactly that wavelength and it is therefore difficult to judge what is getting across. For it is by no means just the words you use which make what you say explicit, it is the inflections, the way you dwell on some words rather than others, your emphasis, and particularly how much energy you let out or hold back, that carries the message. And so much depends on your own state of mind, for how you feel unconsciously colours the voice. Of course this does not happen with people to whom you are close, because of the common ground of understanding, and in any case you so often speak in a kind of shorthand, for much is implicit and does not have to be said. And yet, even with people to whom you are close, misunderstandings arise, because of the way you say something, which can obstruct your underlying motive.

The point is, you do not always realize how much, or how little, you need do to convey the specific whole meaning of what you are saying accurately. In other words, you hear your own voice sub-jectively, coloured by your image of what you think you sound like, and/or what you would like to sound like, and sometimes it is satisfactory and serves your intentions and sometimes it is not. Gradually you come to be more aware of your voice, to assess it objectively and so know what it is telling others, for so often a small adjustment can make all the difference in the world to how you communicate.

2
Good Sound and Good Speaking

Now that we have looked at some of the complexities which condition the voice, we must define what we mean by a good voice. And by that I mean both the sound – or tone – of the voice and the speech.

I think a lot of voice work in the past has been done from a negative point of view – that is to say the emphasis has been on 'correcting' the voice and making it 'better', with all the social and personal implications that the word 'better' contains, somehow implying that you are not quite good enough. The word 'elocution', which voice work is so often called, again has bad associations, with a picture of the teacher imposing something on the pupil – something usually rather precious, some special way of speaking which may not fit the person himself – in other words making him conform to a kind of good behaviour in speaking. Better tone was finding more musical sound, and better speech was usually connected with removing any trace of native accent and sounding perhaps a little 'refined'. I am not saying that all voice work has had this attitude, but there has been enough bad teaching to make people generally wary of voice work in any form, for they quite rightly do not want to sound false, or to inhibit the natural vitality of their own expression.

Good voice work, on the other hand, I believe should always aim to use the voice that is there and stretch it and open up its possibilities, so that it does not limit the personality. We will find that the sound of the voice and the speech relate so much to each other that they are not separate. However, for our own clarity at the moment, we will talk about each separately.

Good Speaking

I believe that speaking well has nothing to do with any kind of standard accent – i.e., BBC, Oxford or 'public school' or whatever you like to call it – but with an awareness of the physical making of words, and forming them completely so that they have their value. Speaking is a physical action – it is the physical means by which you convey what you think and what you feel, and it is therefore important that the physical actions are made firmly and positively.

At the same time we have to be realistic and recognize that our attitudes to speech have been bound up with class and accent, for up until quite recently many jobs have been open only to someone with a standard accent, or at least a person with a standard accent got preference over someone with a regional accent – in other words there has been considerable discrimination – and this, of course, accounts for the negative conformist attitude to the teaching of speech. It not only affected jobs, the whole social mixing of society was very much a class-conscious affair. And we must not, even now, underestimate the bias against accent, for, although class boundaries are rapidly disappearing, a thick accent is still unconsciously equated with lack of education, and it takes a long time for such prejudices to disappear. I am certain that the frustrations that have arisen out of feelings of class inferiority are as important as the frustrations arising out of feelings of sexual inadequacy, and have assumed as much significance in the behaviour of people. If speech is an outward symbol of class, it follows that how you speak is a matter of deep importance to individual self-respect.

Fortunately, as I have said, these barriers are rapidly disappearing. It started back in the '50s and '60s I think, with novels like *Room at the Top* and the plays of John Osborne, such as *Look Back in Anger,* and then with the success of groups like the Beatles and the Rolling Stones and the whole advent of the 'swinging London' scene. The atmosphere suddenly changed, for it seemed that anybody could make money, regardless of background and education, and that they could be socially acceptable. It was quite a remarkable revolution in social attitudes. Of course there is still a small set which hangs on to these class values, but it is interesting to notice that it is now in vogue to speak with a slightly 'off' accent among the trendy upper-class sets. It is not just this kind of trend-setting that has made the difference, that would be belittling it, it is the gradual swing of society as a whole. In the sphere of speech, the BBC itself reflects all these changes, so that now commentators, and those who have become successful personalities on TV, like Frost and Parkinson, no longer conform to any particular way of speaking, though – and this is important – their speech is always vital, alive and clear.

Regarding commentators and reporters in general, their forcefulness is often rather repetitive and overbearing, as I am sure you will have noticed, and this can be irritating. I think it is because they are so aware of the immediacy of the media they are using that, in a sense, that immediacy takes over so that they vocally underline what they are saying. This is particularly true of sports commentators, for instance, though it varies much with the individual. On the whole, I think the news is read extremely well by both the BBC and the commercial companies, with none of the emotive loading that it has in the United States, where a relentless emotional pressure obscures the objective facts and quite certainly acts as a kind of provocateur by adding to people's tensions – in other words, it is far from cool. In the past I think the BBC has played an incredibly important part in making people aware of speech, for in the first years of broadcasting they did try to arrive at a good balance of what was acceptable and what was not, and they found a manner of speech which was educated, but without the extreme distortions of upper class speech, with its nasality and distorted vowel sounds – which are every bit as much an accent as broad Cockney, and in fact have many of the Cockney characteristics – and the speech they arrived at influenced speech all over the country. It is interesting to notice too, how speech goes in fashions, and changes quite noticeably in a short period of time. A recording of a news broadcast of twenty, or even ten, years ago will be markedly different from the speech of a news reader today, and Standard English is changing all the time as any speech which is vital and alive must do. Now, because through the media of radio and television we hear intelligent knowledgeable people being articulate and interesting on all sorts of subjects in all sorts of dialects, the concept that Standard English is the speech of educated people is being scotched – not quite one hundred per cent, but nearly. I think this is marvellous, because there is so much vitality in regional accents and expressions – it is where the language keeps alive.

To speak well, then, is not basically to do with conforming to an accent, but with being intelligible to people you want to reach, so that if an accent is so thick that it cannot be understood outside your own region, then, should you want to use your voice in any sense professionally something obviously has to be done about it. Priests in Ireland, for instance, where regional accents vary very much and are often so thick that they are not intelligible outside their own district, have to find a speech that is acceptable more generally, particularly if their work calls them outside Ireland. Speech is taken very seriously in Irish Catholic Theological Colleges – a young would-be priest can fail his final examinations if his speech is not of the required standard. Again, very strong Scottish accents simply cannot be understood by English people, so that someone who wanted to work in television or radio would be limited to his local station unless he standardized his accent to some degree – and even in business it can be a limitation, particularly if you are dealing with foreign people who can understand English of a fairly standard variety only. An actor, of course, has to be able to speak Standard

English or he would be limited to regional parts — all right if you are from Liverpool and have a run in *Z Cars,* — but actually not practicable!

I feel very strongly that accents should be left alone if in themselves they are clear and do not distort the voice in any way, nor limit the possibilities of the individual. Should you want to standardize your own accent, then that is a matter of individual chŏice, but you should be careful not to iron out the native vitality or impose a kind of pseudo accent on yourself. It is important to arrive at a standard accent through making your own voice clear — the consonants and the vowels — and not by copying someone else's way of speaking. It is a delicate matter, because you must never feel that in any way you are betraying your own background, for then it is bad for you as a person, and something false creeps into the voice — an affectation — it is the motive that matters. For instance, you may enjoy reading Shakespeare and poetry, and if you have the kind of ear that takes this pleasure, you are likely to have equated your own speech naturally to a fairly standard English. (Just as some poetry is written in dialect, as William Barnes's poetry was written in Dorset speech and cannot be read in any other way, so other poetry loses some of its resonance if read in a broad accent.) It is interesting to notice how conditioned and conservative we are to what is seemly and fitting and what is not — for instance, English people cannot quite take the Bible read in an American accent, it is as though it is not quite reverent enough, simply because we have become accustomed to associate American accents with gangsters, Westerns, revivalist meetings and all that goes along with most of the television films we see from over there, and so it does not fit in with talking about God. I am sure that Americans have exactly the same kind of attitude in reverse, and that their reaction to our speech is that it is formal and probably eccentric and effete. Neither of these reactions is logical, but they show what prejudices we have about speech.

A long time ago, when I first started teaching, a firm of horse auctioneers asked me to work with one of their clerks. He was a very bright young man and would therefore be useful to them as an auctioneer, but his speech was not of the right class to be acceptable — the others were all ex-public school. To be fair, he spoke with an almost Dickensian Cockney, substituting 'v's' for 'th's' and *vice versa,* and what is more, could not hear the difference between the sounds. Success involved first training his ear — always a long process — and we spent hours saying things like: 'three thousand three hundred and thirty-three', or 'one-year old foal — two-year old foal' etc., as 'oh' and 'l' sounds were a particularly difficult hurdle for him. Luckily he was not in the least inhibited or resistant to being asked to speak differently. He had to absorb this standard speech so that it felt natural and comfortable, and become sure enough of it so that it could be variable and not sound too good, which meant adjusting his inner ear to the new sounds, and he had to do this without losing the natural vigour of his own speech or sounding self-conscious in any way. Being an uncomplicated person he realised that Standard English was necessary for a better job — a job he would enjoy — and he worked steadily and was successful. A very delicate balance is required to find new sounds comfortable and yet not to lose your own personality in the process. There is always a time-lag between being able to make the new sounds in isolation and then making them part of your own speech.

There is, then, no rule that can be made about accents, it is a matter of individual choice. To my mind, the most important thing to grasp, and what I think so much voice teaching has left out, is the fact that speaking is a physical process, and that good speech has nothing to do with someone else imposing special sounds on you, or with making your speech behave in a particular way and conform to a particular pattern — it is you discovering the feeling of making the sounds themselves — it is you becoming muscularly aware of the movements of the tongue, the lips and the palate, and realising that the more completely you make those movements the more satisfactory and alive your speech will be. For it is those muscular movements that miraculously gather the thoughts and feelings that you want to express and send them out in the shape of words. It is this awareness that will make you feel the energy of the word itself and want to fulfil it — i.e., make the vowels and consonants clearly defined — not by over-emphasis, or by giving each syllable equal weight, but defined in their relative place in the phrase. Because if the lips, tongue and palate are agile, you actually need to do less to make the vowels and consonants clear than if those muscles are stiff and unused to movement. For, and this is most important as I do not want anyone to think it is desirable to mouth words in any way, good speech should not be noticed — we only notice if it is either unclear, or exaggerated in some way. It should always be economical — as soon as you start the exercises you will know exactly what I mean. And you will also find out that the balance between vowels and consonants is very important, especially in relation to filling a large space, because to fill a large space has as much to do with the energy of the word as with the loudness of the sounds.

When you begin to feel this physical life you will find that the words themselves take on an added dimension — a life of their own, and this is where it gets quite exciting — for if you take passages from

Dylan Thomas, for example, where the language is particularly muscular, you will find that the actual commitment to those words when you speak them aloud gives them this added dimension of meaning. You will always find, when working on the voice, that it is at its best when the technical means are forgotten and you are speaking instinctively and responding to the words that you are saying – that is why you should always finish off a session of exercises by speaking something to which you feel committed, the experience of the exercises will remain, but the instinctive response to what you are saying will take over, your imagination will work, and the voice will take on a whole new texture and life of its own. In other words, the voice will always be at its best when the technical means are forgotten and you are free to think about what you are saying, and enjoy saying it.

So 'speaking well' has to do with discovering the vitality of your own speech and having confidence in it, and, through your own physical resources, making it more positive and alive. It is your physical commitment to the words that matters.

Good Sound

By sound I mean the quality or tone of the voice itself – the timbre if you like – and its individuality.

I think everyone has a potentially interesting and rich voice – I mean rich in the variety it can contain – but for all sorts of reasons, some of which we have already looked at, the majority of people do not use this potential. (Of course this only matters if it limits you as a person, and in what you may want to do.) But, as with speech, there are many misconceptions as to what good sound should be, and again I think a lot of this stems from bad teaching. We have all heard the kind of fruity mellifluous voice which sounds 'well-produced', but somehow does not ring quite true. And I do not think it is true, for it is a kind of imposed tone, which comes about when people consciously develop the neck resonance, and push their voice down into the back of the throat where they can hear it sounding deep and having a kind of musicality – there it stays, and of course is limited as to the notes it can use because this kind of tone is tied up with the lower register and perhaps a false assumption that a low voice is more interesting. It is a kind of distortion, for it is not the natural placing for sound, it is self-conscious and you find yourself listening to the sound rather than the words, so that the sound dominates the meaning. The point is it does not spring, it is not alive because it is over-controlled, and it is not a true expression of the person because in some way it is being held on to and made to behave — it therefore reveals nothing of the person behind it. It is also very limited.

What I call a good voice is one that is open and reveals the person. It is when the whole physical being of the person is reflected in the voice, and this happens when you allow yourself to be open to the breath.

Breath is really the all-important factor — how open you are to it and how you use it. Quite simply, if you are relaxed enough to allow the breath to touch down to your centre — i.e., to receive the breath into the deepest part of the chest, so that the diaphragm or floor of the chest takes the breath right down, then, as you release the breath into sound the whole of your chest cavity will add its vibrations and resonance and contribute to the sound. It is then that your whole body becomes part of the sound, giving it solidity, firmness and edge. And, instead of sounding what I call 'voicey' and mellifluous and 'beautiful', it will sound more positive, more individual, and more you — for it is simply that you are using the whole of yourself to make sound more fully. To begin with you may feel you are working harder, but in fact it will be the opposite, for once you have found the exact placing of the breath and the ability to use the breath fully to make sound, you will find you need less breath to make the tone carry and the process will be more economical. The voice will spring of its own impulse — like loosing an arrow. It actually becomes easier.

Let me put it another way. If the breathing is shallow and only happens in the upper part of the chest, besides making for tension in the shoulders and the neck, you will find the voice only starts from there and the possibilities of resonance from the rest of your body are cut off. The voice then will always sound high, whatever actual pitch you are using, and somehow cut off, and the tone will be thin. It is rather like playing a melody on a piano without any chords in the bass — the tune sounds high, but once you put in the accompanying base chords, the tune sounds deeper and has, of course, more resonance. This analogy goes for the voice — if there is no resonance from the chest and neck resonators the voice will sound higher in pitch than it actually is, and very thin. It is interesting to notice that this quality of sound often appears with rather intellectual people, or people who are emotionally not very open. But the point is that if the voice is springing only from the upper part of the chest, it does not reflect the whole physical presence of the person. If you receive the breath right down to your centre, root it, providing you are not tense and that you can get the sense of the voice starting from the point to which the breath has touched down, then a) your whole chest will contribute to the sound, giving you gratuitous resonance which you do not have to work for but which is just there; b) it will reflect your physical presence, and c) it will have a vitality and definition of its own. And, far from being the generalized 'good' tone of the plummy or over-conscious sort, you will have a sound which is particular to you, and therefore more distinctive. It is actually good sense.

Also, if the breath is the impulse to the sound in this manner, it frees the pitch range in a quite astonishing way, and you will find yourself using notes in your voice that you did not know you had, both in pitch and in quality. In other words, and this is what is important, it opens up the possibilities of the voice, so that it will be more interesting because you have found more to use, and once you hear this range in your voice you instinctively want to use it. This is when it becomes an exciting and also a liberating experience. This is what exercises are about — they are not important in the sense that you can do them — they matter because through them you will experience more sounds, which you will then unconsciously start using in your everyday life, for they will feel right in that they are more responsive to what you have to say — more textured in fact.

It is not only the chest that can contribute to the sound. As we have already said, if the neck is free and not tense — and so con-stricted — the resonating space there, which is called the pharynx, contributes much to the sound you make and enriches it. The space at the back of the tongue, the mouth, the nose, the hollow spaces in the head and the bones of the skull, all can add their own vibrations, providing the jaw, the palate and the tongue are free and allow the sounds to be open. Also, and this is something which is often missed, the consonants themselves can add their own vibrations if the muscles involved in forming them make firm enough muscular contact. For instance in a voiced consonant such as 'd', if the tip of the tongue makes firm enough contact with the hard palate you will feel a vibration here; or with 'b', if the muscles in the lips make good firm contact the 'b' will spring off with a certain vibration; or with 'z', if the tip of the tongue is pressing firmly enough against the teeth you can feel the tongue tingle and that means it is carrying its own vibration. All these sounds can be made quite defined, yet with hardly any vibration. But when muscular firmness is there and those consonants contain their own vibration it gives another dimension to the voice — it is also vital to the placing of the tone in the front of the mouth by helping to keep the vowels forward, and is vital to the carrying power or projection of the voice.

So you see, sound can be found in all parts of the body, and once you are aware of it through quite simple exercises, you will find you can actually place the sound quite easily by consciously thinking of it in those areas.

Obviously there will always be some difference in range between a man's voice and a woman's voice — the pitch range of a man is on the whole lower than that of a woman and has a certain difference in quality. However, this does not prevent a man extending his upper register if he has a deep voice, or a woman extending her lower register if her voice is high. When extending the upper register, always remain conscious of the possible chest resonance that you have so that you keep the richness behind the note, and, when extending the range down, consciously keep the head and face resonance focussed so that you keep a brilliance and definition in the sound.

I would like here to say a few things about singing. Singing is, of course, an excellent way to stretch the voice. It strengthens the breathing and makes you find the resonances I have been talking about, perhaps in a slightly different way, but it certainly makes you experience them. However, I think it is important to recognize the difference between exercising, or training the voice for singing, and training it for speaking, for the actual focus or placing is different. For both you need to open up the breathing and all the resonating cavities, but for singing you convey your meaning through the disciplines of sound and all its nuances — the sound is the message — so that the energy is in the resonance. The singer needs all the resonance he can find, and though obviously the words have an importance, it is through the sound — the resonance — that he ulti-mately expresses himself, and it is the resonance that contains his energy. Whereas with the speaker, he wants what resonance he can find, but in the end his energy must be with the word, for it is the word containing all his thought and all his feeling that he wants to convey. This is why we have always to be careful of the balance of head resonance — if you only feel a generalized resonance in the mask or front of the face the words will not impinge, but if all the resonance you find backs up the word and, as it were, is sent out by the word, then the focus will be right.

Good sound, comes from the development of your own vocal resources, extending and enriching it and making the sound more particular to you. Although you will feel benefit from the exercises almost immediately, it will take time before you begin to feel it coming naturally into your everyday use — and this is right, because it must be a process of discovery, a discovery of what your voice can do for you, and not by imposing any way of speaking on yourself.

3
Breathing and Relaxation

I certainly believe that good breathing is the key to a good voice, for nothing will work quite right unless the breathing is working right for you. If we remember that it is the breath which is the initiator of the sound – i.e., the force that strikes the vocal cords causing them to vibrate – it follows that the firmer that force of breath is, the truer the sound will be. And by good breathing I do not mean using a lot of breath, but using the breath properly to make sound.

As soon as you start the exercises you will see that 'rooting' the voice to the 'centre' and letting the breath 'touch down' is not vague mystical jargon, but an action that you can feel positively. When you exercise the muscles between the ribs, which contract and so draw the ribs out, you get an increased expansion of the rib cage. This action also stretches the diaphragm and pulls it out and flattens it – for the diaphragm is a dome-shaped sheet of muscle which acts as the floor of the chest. As the diaphragm flattens it descends and draws air into the deeper part of the chest. The diaphragm is also attached to the stomach muscles and so, by allowing the stomach muscles to give way, the diaphragm can descend even lower and draw the breath right down into the stomach. To begin with you feel this by exercising the muscles involved and becoming conscious of where they are. It seems to be only a muscular movement – ultimately, however, it should not feel muscular, or in any way a contrived movement, it should simply feel that you are drawing your breath down to your centre, and then releasing it into sound, as if you were tapping the sound out like a drum. In ordinary life you are not conscious of making movement to breathe, nor should you be when taking the breath in more deeply, but you will find it extraordinary that simply by thinking in terms of touching the breath down to your centre, you will actually start to do it. The action goes with the thought.

So good breathing is fundamental on two levels. Firstly because, as we have seen, by taking the breath down to your centre the whole chest will contribute to the sound and make it fuller, richer and more expansive. But also because, as I said at the beginning, if you take time to breathe you actually feel your physical weight as a person, you become calmer and you take time to receive and think –

it therefore makes you more confident. Ideally your voice is a statement of yourself and for this reason it must be part of your whole physical being. And, of course, good breathing is healthy.

But I think there is something even more to it than this. It is in your stomach – guts – that physical responses to basic feelings such as fear, anger, pleasure, take place – we know that actual anatomical changes take place in response to our emotions and states of being, so that if we are nervous or frightened we have varying degrees of response, from butterflies in the stomach to a desire to defecate, we also feel excitement in the stomach. It follows, therefore, that if we take the breath into that centre it is then in touch with these emotional responses and part of them, the voice then becomes part of our emotional self as well as our physical and thinking self, and reflects that self. And further, and perhaps the most important thing of all, firm breathing helps to stabilize that centre, and so there is a two-way thing here, for the breathing reacts on the emotional self and strengthens it. This is not by any means a new thought, obviously many people feel benefit from practising deep breathing, from whatever point of view they do it – breathing plays an integral part in the practice of Yoga, for instance – but for the person wishing to make the best of his voice, it has all these levels of significance.

It is interesting to notice how, when you are in a relaxed state of mind, your breathing is easy and you are not aware of it, but as soon as you become nervous or frightened the pattern alters immediately and becomes quick and shallow. Certainly the depth of people's breathing varies enormously from person to person, and even with the individual himself, because the breath relates totally to your state of mind. There are times when you are in a state of anxiety and you feel that it is impossible to take deep breaths. This can last for quite a long period of time – but by doing exercises regularly, you can gradually break the pattern and become more at ease altogether. I think most people go through such periods at one time or another, and breathing well has a very stabilizing effect. It also helps to brace oneself against difficulty – there is often much truth in old sayings, and if you have anything difficult to do or say one is told to take a deep breath and get on with it – how good, then, for the breathing to be strong all the time. I am convinced that openness to breath gives you strength.

I think also that the way you use breath is indicative of the kind of person you are – if you let a lot of breath gush out so that the voice sounds breathy and out of control, it possibly indicates that you, as a person, feel you have to give out everything and keep no strength in reserve for yourself – perhaps too generous – and this

35

can mean that you do not feel wholly your right to be you, it is as if you need to justify being. On the other hand it can indicate an opposite – i.e., that you feel you are ungenerous but would like to seem generous. Using too little breath can also indicate certain things, like being cautious or timid, or not committing yourself completely as a person. Or the opposite again, it may mean that you are afraid to let out your feelings because you feel they may take over and become out of control. These of course are generalized prognoses, hints and suggestions to make you aware of just how completely the voice and the person are tied up. You start then to be aware of the voice in a different way – first in others and then in yourself. One thing is certain, the surer you are of your own self – and I do not mean over-confident, but rather self-accepting – the more authority the voice will have without being over-emphatic.

One cannot help but come to the conclusion that the high-pitched insensitive voice that carries across restaurants and railway compartments, so that you are forced to listen to it, comes from a person who, as it were, has cut himself off from his feelings, who does not want to know what is going on inside himself, and who therefore has to project himself on other people and draw their attention.

The physical action of breathing to your centre, I am sure, actually makes you more aware of your centre and so of your self.

But all this can only work if you are as free from tension as possible – and I suppose it is tension, both physical and mental that holds us up most, it seems to be almost the normal condition of life today, and something of which most people are aware.

By tension of course I mean unnecessary tension, for there has to be tension to make any movement at all – just to stand upright requires certain sets of muscles to be tensed to keep you in that position. That is good tension, for muscles need to be toned up and ready for movement. Slack, over-relaxed muscles make for bad posture and bad movement. What we are concerned with is unnecessary tension – how often when you are sitting in a train or bus, driving a car, writing, knitting, reading, doing whatever odd job, if you stop for a moment you suddenly realise that your shoulders are tensed and that you are holding them a good inch above their normal relaxed position – that tension is doing nothing, for you could do what you are doing without them being tensed at all. Energy is going into the shoulders to keep them braced to no purpose – it is therefore energy wasted. People get tense like this in various parts of the body – some people get a lot of tension in the legs, others in the back, others in the stomach, but probably most common, is tension in the upper part of the back and in the shoulders and neck, and of course it is this tension that affects the voice most, for tension in the back constricts the breathing, and tension in the shoulders and neck constricts the resonating spaces and so limits the voice.

Few people, I think, realize just how acutely responsive the voice is to tension, for tension comes when you are about to speak — so often when you get ready to speak there is a slight forward movement of the chin and something braces in the neck and fixes, and so becomes tense. I have noticed this time and time again when giving people voice classes. I can work with someone, getting them absolutely relaxed on the floor, where there is not even tension needed to hold a position, I have got the arms, back, shoulders, neck all quite free, and then, purposely, have started to talk to them about odd things such as what they are going to do later and when they begin to reply immediately something happens in the neck — it braces somewhere and tension comes. It is quite fascinating. How much more, then, is this likely to happen when the speaking you are about to do is important and the circumstances are likely to produce tension.

Research has been done on this reaction of the neck with people who stammer, and here this reaction is very pronounced, but the point is, it happens to some extent with everyone. One's mood and state of being reflects in the voice — if you are tired or depressed you actually feel as though some part of your voice has cut out. Over the telephone, for instance, you can detect the mood of someone you know well immediately — you can tell if it has more or less of its normal vitality, whether the inflections are alive or dull; if they are excited you hear the extra vitality in the voice. You can certainly tell immediately by the voice whether someone is at ease or not. There are, at the moment, tests being made on sophisticated equipment which can detect whether someone is lying, by measuring inaudible hints of stress in the voice — that is to say the voice sounds no different when it is lying, but there is stress in the voice which can be measured electronically. This of course is not to do with us, but it is interesting in that it shows just how totally the voice is part of one's being. Tests also show that measurement of vocal vibrations can identify as accurately as fingerprints.

On another tack altogether, the same firm of auctioneers who had asked me to help with the Cockney accent, also asked me to help two of their junior partners, who had no accent trouble, but whose voices got excessively tired when doing their job for longish periods — they have to talk in the open, and though there is mechanical aid from microphones it is still a tiring business, for you get no comeback when speaking outside and it is difficult to judge what is getting through, therefore the tendency is to push the voice and strain it. Both men were upper class with rather stilted accents, and their necks were very tense. A lot of work had to be done to get the necks free so that the voices could come out without strain. One of them in particular was extremely sensitive about this. To get his neck moving freely I had to get him to take his stiff collar off, and he found it very difficult to drop his neck forward and back and roll it round. He had quite a few lessons and was getting on well, and we were on good terms, yet one day as we were doing the same routine head-rolling exercises, he suddenly went very red and said: 'I can't stand it any longer', and rushed out. The next day, to show there was no ill feeling, he sent me a very splendid table lamp. The important thing to me was that I learnt just how incredibly vulnerable people are to knowledge of their own tensions and their own voices, and that there are moments when they cannot bear that knowledge. It taught me a great lesson about how much care one has to take when dealing with voice or accent, and how easily a person's ego can be disturbed by unthinking criticism, and how constantly alive you must be to each person's individual sensitivity. I just had not realized to what extent the young man's tension in the neck was a part of his protective armour — and everyone has protective armour of one sort or another.

The story also clearly shows that some physical tension comes from a deeper level of anxiety than can be dealt with here, that, of course, you will realize. For the most part, however, physical tension comes from the normal stress and strain of everyday life and much can be done about it. If you can break the pattern of physical tension it helps to ease the mental tension which is causing it — it is again a two-way process — one helps the other. Through simple exercises, making you aware of what is happening in different sets of muscles, you become conscious of where and when you get tense, and through these exercises you can put yourself in a state of being 'free'. I think 'free' is an important word, for I prefer that term to 'relaxed'. To be relaxed implies slackness and heaviness which is not at all what we want, and also that state can transfer to tension immediately you start to move. Whereas to be 'free' implies a state of non-tension which is at the same time ready for action — in other words alert, but not tense. And it is important that you can feel each part separately free, so that when you move one part of yourself another part does not become sympathetically tense — i.e., only the muscles involved should have tension. Now by making yourself familiar with this state of freedom, it becomes a positive state which you can acquire at will, and not just the negative state of not being tense. It is not then a question of not being tense, it is a question of being free, and there is all the difference in the world between these two attitudes. For instance, if I asked you to clench your fist you would not have to think first about how to do it, you would just do it, and it is the same with being free — you need to get so familiar with the sensation of being free that you can put yourself into that state at will without thinking about how to do it. Thus, the moment you are aware of being tense, you can make yourself free.

We can learn to free ourselves from the physical tensions that we get in ordinary everyday life, and when you start the exercises I think you will find it easier than you imagine. Then you can begin to control all the extra tensions you get in the particular situations that make you nervous — for it is these situations that emphasize the normal tensions. Two things are important to say here. Firstly, that when you become extra nervous — when the nerves take over in fact — you do not function so efficiently, you do not think so quickly, you do not listen so accurately — tension has a paralyzing effect to some extent or other. You always feel that your own nerves are the most crippling because your concentration is turned inwards into yourself, and your energy is being short-circuited, as it were, and is not being productive. Because you are preoccupied with yourself, you do, in fact, isolate yourself and cut yourself off from the energy which can come from other people and sustain you. Secondly, we must remember that some nervous energy is a good thing, it makes the adrenalin flow and the mind work quicker, and in any case to be nervous shows you care. Nervous energy is a different thing from nervous tension — one produces energy (which always has to be paid for!) and the other wastes it.

Briefly then, by first recognizing, and then controlling our physical tension, we relieve to some extent the causes of tension, and we are also able to control the voice and do more with it, which in itself is a freeing process and makes for better communication. We all have anxiety, we all have tension — some anxiety takes years to come to terms with — but a lot of tension can be dealt with quite easily and simply, and it is within everyone's capability to do so.

4
Communication and Words

I want to stop thinking about voices subjectively for a bit — i.e., how you use them and how they sound — and look at our means of communication — words. Because we use them all the time, we take them for granted and do not think about them. But I think there are several interesting things we can learn if we think for a moment about our attitude to them, how we use them, and their importance to us.

It seems to me that words are at once the most primitive and the most sophisticated things we possess. They started out as primitive sounds to express needs of survival and have developed into a most advanced means of communication, able to express degrees of sensibility, complex philosophical and legal argument, and all kinds of terminology and jargon essential for the understanding of every science there is. This is quite a thought, for their primitive need is still with us.

In reality, the majority of people are very limited in the vocabulary they use and partly this is so because in ordinary life not very much demand is made on us, or, put another way, we can get by without a large vocabulary. Yet part of being able to express yourself well in public has to do with confidence and ability in using words, so we should be continually questioning the words we use and our accuracy in their use. There is great joy, I think, in extending your vocabulary, but it is something that has to be cultivated.

I suppose we use words to cover two areas — a) to communicate information, and b) to relate or express experience, and this latter can take us into several levels of understanding. I will try to make this clear, by relating three quite different incidents showing reactions to words. They are quite small incidents, but show something of the way words work on us.

We are concerned with being able to communicate accurately and easily with other people, but easily does not necessarily mean talking a lot, for we tend to mistrust people who find it too easy to use words — it is not a good thing to be glib. Not long ago I was taking part in a symposium for a group of teachers at an American college. There were two American actors and myself taking part in the symposium — grand word! — and the subject was: 'What did

Shakespeare mean to each of us'. The actors of course answered in terms of their work as actors, and I talked about Shakespeare's use of language. I was explaining that Shakespeare used language to express exactly and completely what was being thought and felt at the moment — that is to say that the action is in the words, and the words reveal what is happening at the time — i.e., the words are the action. When Hamlet soliloquises: 'To be, or not to be — that is the question;' he is discovering at that moment something about existence and non-existence — it is an act of discovery about himself. In all Shakespeare the action is revealed in the word — the words are explicit. And I went on to say that this was what made Shakespeare different from modern plays, for playwrights now very often use language as a disguise for what is going on underneath, in the sub-text, as we call it. I then added — and this is the relevant part — that I feel this to be true of our lives today, that we tend to use language to cover up what we feel, rather than to reveal what we feel; it is a kind of over-civilization. And an extraordinary thing happened: one young teacher — I suppose in his mid-twenties — got up and with great sincerity asked what he should do because he did not trust words any more. The exact dialogue went like this:

Questioner: How do you play Shakespeare for people who no longer believe in words?

Myself: How can you not believe in words?

Questioner: To a large extent I don't. When you've heard statements from presidential aides that a certain statement is no longer 'operative' when, in fact, this statement was and is a bare-faced lie, I don't believe in words any more. They're so misused, and they're so used to disguise feelings and meanings that I really don't trust words any more. How do you reach somebody like me?

Myself: *You're* going to have a hard time. (I regretted this flippancy.)

Questioner: If I thought it was a personal thing I would say 'yeah' and sit down. But I'm not alone. I only have to look at my students in the university to see a whole sea of faces that no longer believe in words either.

And this was to me a chilling moment, for he was right — it was a terrible indictment of the printed and verbal diarrhoea which we expect and accept every day of our lives. Of course he was referring specifically to the whole public relations jargon used in the Watergate cover-up, whence came an entire new vocabulary and phraseology, sinister in the fact that it seems to have little to do with reality. And indeed it came out of the need to bend reality. For it is true that the more a person wishes to conceal, the wordier he becomes – to be wordy both tires and confuses. You cannot trust language like that, and that is what he was protesting about. This, you will say, is a specifically American case, but I am not so sure – I think we hear echoes of this kind of public relations jargon here in our political and public fields, and the disillusion we feel for politics has something to do with the way politicians talk to us. But it is not only in politics that we are conscious of this bloated language – newspapers, magazines, television talk programmes, advertizements have to fill time and space with words, whether it be about sport, film personalities, aftershave lotion or art, so that in the end words lose their value. Continually, when reading a newspaper or listening to television, I notice the use of an unusual word – always used intellectually and significantly – and very soon you find that word has caught on and become common usage – 'charisma' is one word I can think of which sprang into prominence some years ago together with 'life-style', both high-sounding words making you believe that whoever was speaking was saying something quite special – in the end they are used so often that they signify, if not nothing, certainly very little. A phrase like 'in fact', now so common, seems to be used to con the listener into thinking that what is being said is intellectually deeply thought out – it is usually an unnecessary phrase. It is a kind of 'gamesmanship' with words. Football commentators talk about players who 'read' the game well – what does this mean?

We are all guilty of this at some time or another – I have carefully gone through this book cutting out many 'in fact's'. The point I want to make, is that we choose the words we use, and so it follows that the choice of those words indicates something about us. We should, therefore, choose with care. If a person chooses to use five words instead of one – 'at that point in time', instead of 'then' – it tells us something about that person and of the society that accepts this. Just as the rather bizarre shorthand slang of the RAF during the war, with its schoolboy war-games flavour, told us about the attitude they found it necessary to adopt to deal with the situations they had to face every day. This went to the opposite extreme of understatement. Today we have become accustomed to language which lacks simplicity – a bad sign – which is blown-up, over-emotional and sensational, a language which 'escalates' reactions. And this is particularly dangerous when it concerns reportage of news – the news 'media' as it is now called, for it can only add to the disturbance we feel around us. Also with us is the vocabulary of the computer, a whole new language, dehumanized, orientated to machines and not to people, which has a nasty way of creeping into our everyday communication.

All we can do is try to be accurate, and use words with care. I say 'accurate' rather than 'honest', deliberately, for pride in our own honesty can be deluding. These six lines from T.S. Eliot's *Burnt Norton* rather sum it up:

> Words strain,
> Crack and sometimes break, under the burden,
> Under the tension, slip, slide, perish,
> Decay with imprecision, will not stay in place,
> Will not stay still. Shrieking voices
> Scolding, mocking, or merely chattering,
> Always assail them.

The next thing I want to say about words is this. The ability to express thoughts and feelings precisely matters at a deep level which has to do with the relief and satisfaction of having said what you wished to say with accuracy. A great deal of tension or 'aggro' builds up inside you when you feel you cannot express truly what matters to you – this relates to both personal and business relationships. Of course it is necessary sometimes to suppress what you feel, but there are many times when you want to be explicit, but because of lack of confidence in your ability to be clear you become tense and it comes out wrong. Once you sense this happening you stop taking your time, you stop choosing your words, you lose reasoning and control, and it becomes an emotional issue with yourself. By then what you wanted to say has become out of proportion and inaccurate. We are all familiar with situations where you come away wishing that you had said either more, or less! This may sound trivial, but I believe it to be of deep importance to the growth of the individual that he feels capable of being articulate about his feelings – not over-emotional, just articulate. Whether you are, or are not, able to be articulate most certainly springs from childhood. In business and trade disputes I am certain much rancour springs from frustration with yourself for not having said what you had intended. This comes out of confidence in yourself as a person, but your trust in your voice, and the time you allow yourself to take, can only increase that confidence – and is part of it. Above all, it is the belief that what you have to say is valid, for you can only be confident about what you believe in. The incident I want to relate here is actually a second-hand one, but it makes what I have just said clear. A long time ago I remember listening to Emanuel Shinwell being interviewed on television, and one thing he said stuck in my mind. The interviewer had asked him something like what was his secret for keeping so healthy and mentally alert at his age, and Lord Shinwell replied to the effect that it was because he·

believed in speaking his mind. Now this, of course, has much to do with the individual temperament and the depth of a person's convictions, for he was not suggesting plain speaking from any shallow motive — i.e., he did not mean speaking without restraint — what he did mean was the sense of release he got from saying what he felt to be right. Lord Shinwell has a gift for words and enjoys using them, it is part of his trade, so he has an innate freedom with them that others have to work for — but the freedom to say all you intend is what we are after.

We can take this point much deeper. Actually speaking certain words in some circumstances can be upsetting, the act of bringing feelings to the surface via words may be disturbing or painful — the feelings may be of pride, happiness, anger, or shame — if they are deeply felt, they are difficult to speak about, but, and this is important, speaking about them changes them. The feeling is different after you have spoken about it. Words themselves are an active force — I think we can all recognise this experience. Speaking about the feeling makes it objective as well as subjective. They say 'A trouble shared is a trouble halved' — speaking about it puts it in perspective. Talking about someone you love gives them an image which is not only private. To talk about something you have done wrong actually helps to cleanse you, the more difficult it is to talk about, the more cleansed you feel afterwards — you 'get if off your chest', or you 'get it out of your system', or it is a 'weight off your mind' — all those marvellously organic phrases which show just how closely the mind and the body are interrelated. This is why the act of confession must be a releasing experience, something which releases you physically as well as mentally. Words can heal. Speaking accurately about one's feelings can hurt. The third from last line of *King Lear,* spoken by Edgar, holds much validity:

'Speak what we feel, not what we ought to say.'

I hope this brings home clearly just how potent words are in our conscious and subconscious mind. Certainly they have strong associations for us in the Freudian sense, for every slip of the tongue tells a story. These associations spring from our early, private, emotional experiences. Things said to frighten a child into being 'good' remain — the words stick and so will always have a reference to those fears, even though you have rationalized the fears themselves. Words like 'naughty', 'dirty', 'wicked', said to a child will remain in association with what they were referring to for a lifetime. So this third point is really about what effect words have on us.

I remember once teaching a high-ranking Army officer who was going to read the lesson at a cathedral service in the presence of the Queen. It was a special occasion and he wanted to do his best. He came three times to work on the reading. We did a good deal of work, not on the actual passage, but on breathing and relaxation, projection and phrasing, and practised on other prose. At first his reading was stilted and tense, but he quickly caught on to the reason for the exercises and soon became much freer. The passage he was reading happened to be the Beatitudes which includes the phrase: 'Blessed are the pure in heart, etc.,', and at the third and last lesson it really sounded good — easy phrasing, clear and with the right things picked out. I told him so and said it sounded good except for one word — and he immediately said: 'I know, the word pure'. He was right, because he pronounced it as 'pyer', cut very short and said right in the back of his throat, so that it was not easily recognizable. He then told me that he found the word actually hard to say, because he remembered things about his schooldays which he felt were not pure and he still had a hang-up over the word. I thought this remarkable, firstly, because it showed how words are tied up with experience, and secondly, because he had recognized it himself and was so open as to tell me. It impressed me a lot.

So far we have talked about three things — the care we should take with words, the importance of saying accurately what we feel, and how words work on us. I would like to take this last point further — it is an interesting thing that the actual voicing of words makes them take on another dimension of meaning. I will try to make this clear.

Children like saying nursery rhymes, the rhythm and sound of them is satisfying. We do not lose this pleasure when we grow up — there is an atavistic pleasure in the rhythm and sound of words, which is presumably what is left over from the excitement of the primitive chants and prayers that used to be said round elderberry trees or whatever. There is magic in chants, and we are still affected by them. The nursery rhyme *Ring a ring o' roses* we now know was said as a kind of charm against the plague. Privately we often speak the name of someone we love aloud — there is something about voicing the name which is necessary to us.

Let me try to collect these thoughts in dramatic terms. Every actor who plays Hamlet will speak the soliloquy 'To be, or not to be' differently, because every actor investigating those lines will have his lifetime of experience, which is unique to him, to draw on, so that those lines will have different associations for him than for another actor, and so call forth different reactions. The lines are about existence and the possibility of non-existence, and pose a question which is implicit in each person's own life. When an actor speaks those lines, they will take on the levels of awareness that that actor has and he will illuminate them accordingly. The words also have power in themselves, and will react on the hearer in different ways and at differing levels of understanding. Someone who has considered the possibility of suicide will react in a different way from someone who has never questioned his own existence — possibly the more one loves life the more present the possibility of non-existence is. But that is only one level — the argument of the speech. There are other levels, for the speech uses words in a certain rhythm and with a certain eloquence — we call it heightened language — and the sound of the speech works on people. I think everyone has certain pieces of poetry which they like and enjoy repeating — heightened language which in some way satisfies us without our quite knowing why. It is not necessarily classic poetry, there are tremendously good lyrics written to contemporary pop music which have the same need to be repeated — Bob Dylan for example; the words stick in your mind. We do not know why this is, but this enjoyment of the sound of words can take us into another territory — the associations of words and rhythms can penetrate the subconscious understanding. Speaking those lines of Hamlet aloud can make them mean something quite particular to you, and quite different from listening to an actor interpreting them for you.

The number of quotations from Shakespeare that we use in every-day speech is astonishing, and even everyday clichés that we use like 'time heals', we speak as though the speaking of it had power. The funeral service — whether you believe in Christianity or not — with its 'ashes to ashes and dust to dust' has reverberations within us which move us without our understanding why. We use it as a symbol and the using of it helps to relieve our feelings. Actually physically committing yourself to the words releases an area of feeling in you.

I think we also get the same kind of pleasure out of using slang, which has novelty and wit in which we can all participate. Dialect speech too has marvellously rich expressions — the Yorkshire 'I'll have your guts for garters' is one that sticks in my mind. But we must remember that slang springs from an attitude of mind — the wit of Cockney slang which has to make light of hard times — the kind of slang which came out of Negro blues, which originated in the Negroes singing a kind of code to each other, in the cotton plantations, that was not intelligible to the white master — in the same way, the slang which has come out of the drug 'scene' was a code language to cover its illicit use. But as with so many things, the slang catches on and becomes trendy and in a way second-hand; it then starts to be a kind of uniform, like faded jeans, behind which we hide our individual identity of feeling. Like everything else it can suffer from over-exposure. It can be a cliché — it depends completely on the attitude of the person using it.

This, I suppose, is the key to it all, for it is your attitude to words that give them their possibility of life and wit — it is continually being aware of what they can do and how their meaning can shift in different contexts, and not being afraid to use them. This has nothing to do with class or education, for some upper class speech is very stilted and full of habitually repetitive words like 'frightfully' and 'awfully' which makes speech just as uncommunicative as when every other word is 'fucking' — all three words are devalued and have become boring.

I think it interesting that much upper-class and supposedly-educated English speech is stilted both in vocabulary and diction — i.e., the placing of the speech is made back in the mouth with little muscular commitment from the lips and front of the tongue and the jaw is often stiff. Faulty 'r' sounds, for instance, are more common in upper than in lower-class speech. I am sure that this has much to do with the fact that children of wealthy parents are put in the care of nannies as babies, so that their closest emotional tie is with the nanny and not the parent. Further, the nanny occupies the dual role of being at the same time in charge of the child and yet an employee, so not the equal of the child. The relationship for the child is not a simple one. Later he is sent to boarding school where his very ordinary fears and loneliness cannot be allowed to come to the surface. The basic question which a child is continually asking — 'Do you love me?', cannot be answered in those circumstances and so there is no reassurance. So, I do not think it an accident that we get speech which says 'womb' instead of 'room', whereas working-class speech is probably more outgoing and physically committed, and a lot more colourful — perhaps more creative in language. The muscular commitment to speech that, say, a docker or a meat-porter has when he is angry is apparent — 'fuck off' can carry powerful physical force. This is not by any means a flippant comment, because that is a relish so often lacking in educated speech — yet if you read aloud any passage from one of Shaw's plays, which are packed with thought and argument, you can hear just how physically alive educated language can be.

Fundamentally it is using language to express our attitude to life, not in order to be polite. Perhaps it is just being more honest.

I do not know what the equivalents to these examples would be in American speech. I have noticed that New York speech is vital and original, whereas other American speech appears to be over-relaxed, somehow signalling in the voice that 'everything is under control', and it does not seem quite true. Other American speech I have noticed seems to signal 'I am intellectual', which again is not quite believable. I know a lot gives the impression of being over-wordy with a pretention to culture. So one concludes that in some way they do not want to seem ordinary — or is it the ordinary things they do not want to look at. They seem to shore themselves up against reality with words. Obviously the same things happen as in English speech, it is just that the actual vowel and consonant sounds are different.

One of the best ways of developing your vocabulary and habit of words is by reading good prose aloud, and listening for its simplicity, economy and power. If it is good writing, you will find all the words are necessary.

In the end you have to be true to yourself, but each one of us is interesting because each one of us is unique, therefore what we have to say is unique.

5
Your Voice

People are always asking me to tell them what is wrong with their voice. Not so long ago, I was being interviewed on radio about my work, and how I go about teaching people. It was actually a record programme with requests and some chat in between the records. The person who ran the programme wanted to read one of the request cards over the air, and then have me tell him what was wrong with the way he did it, and the correct way to do it (anyway, I suspected he was going to put on a funny voice) and I told him I could not do it, at which he was rather upset and obviously thought I was being difficult. But I was not, for he did this job every day perfectly well, so what was there to say? No voice is wrong if it is communicating adequately, and I would hate to feel that that is what people think. You cannot think of the voice apart from the person – it *is* the person speaking. There is no correct way of reading anything, for each person will respond in a different way to the same passage – each person's experience is different, therefore each person's frame of reference is different.

You cannot divorce the voice from the person, or the job that person requires his voice to do. Each person reading this book will want something different out of it, and hopefully will get what he wants.

As I said to begin with, the voice is a statement of yourself – it is 'I am', therefore, for you to feel you are getting the most out of it, it must be physically part of your whole self. If you become aware of the parts of the body involved in using the voice and speaking, it will be that. For just as an athlete goes into training to get his muscles to the required efficiency, or a pianist exercises his fingers to make them more agile, so you can exercise the voice to get just what you want out of it. You want to be able to rely on it so that it is strong enough to carry in the space you are using, without strain, or showing nerves, and with clarity. If you have much public speaking to do, you want to know how to handle it, so that it is interesting in itself and is flexible and not boring. You want sufficient command over words and vocabulary, so that you have the confidence to express yourself in any situation – firmness without aggression, precision without pedantry. You want to be clear and intelligible, and you want to open up its possibilities. All these things the exercises can help you to achieve. I suspect when you ask what is wrong with your voice, it really boils down to two things — a) you feel you are not getting as much out of your voice as you could, and that when you are conscious of it you get tense, and b) you need reassurance, as we all do.

The good thing about doing the exercises and working on the voice is that you can feel when it is better — you know when it feels right and true. This is most important, for you develop your own judgement, and reassurance from other people becomes less necessary.

Exercises are a means to find the mixture of mental and physical preparedness that we need if the voice is to be at its best.

There are three more things I would like to say before we get on to the exercises. The first is about 'signalling' — I used this word in the last chapter, and it concerns not what we are saying but our manner in saying it, and by this I mean we frequently try to put in our voice our attitude to a situation. Let me explain. If we feel sympathy towards someone, we not only say what we feel to that person we also try to put something in the voice — an excess of sympathy — to underline what we are feeling, as though we did not recognize that what we were saying was enough, or that being sympathetic was enough. Also it has an adverse effect on the person with whom we are sympathizing, oddly enough it belittles him — I think we shy away from being sympathized with, for basically we do not like sympathy as it puts us in an inferior position. Another example is that when people are anxious to get something across, they frequently get over-emphatic and this is tiring, so we retreat from it. We all know the person who comes very close when they talk, and as you try to back away they come forward until finally you are cornered. This is an extreme example, but if, when speaking in public, you get too emphatic or aggressive, the instinct of the listener is to retreat, and in the end switch off. Any excess is irritating and we tend to shy away. So we need to be on the look-out for these tendencies in ourselves — it is always easy to see the faults in other people, but to see them in ourselves requires great honesty. I know, for instance, that I have a tendency to over-explain, because I do not trust my ability to get things across sufficiently. I know I also tend to want people to respond more than I should expect, so that if I am giving a talk I find myself saying 'do you understand?', or 'does that make sense?', yet if I were on the other end — i.e., listening, I would not feel it necessary to respond, I would want to be left alone to listen and take it in. It is this question of needing reassurance. Another thing people tend to signal is 'I understand what you feel and I am your equal' — a kind of over-sympathy which actually sounds just patronizing, like talking down to children. Do not be ashamed of knowing more than someone you are talking to. One simply has to be watchful about one's habits. Certainly, any over-statement is irritating to the listener, and if you are doing a lot of speaking in public you need sometimes to put yourself in the position of the audience and try to imagine what they are receiving.

This happens in an extreme way at interviews for jobs, where you feel you have to present the whole of yourself at one go — of course this is impossible, you can only present yourself at that moment in that situation. But if you are calm and firm, that should be enough — beware of signalling over-willingness. Inevitably, when you are with people you do not know a certain formality creeps in, mainly in the kind of words you use, as though the voice is on its best behaviour . . . perhaps subservience.

The second thing we should consider is listening. In everyday life I believe we listen much less accurately than we would care to admit. Because we are so caught up with what we are thinking and feeling ourselves, we are often preparing for what we are going to say or do after we have finished listening — perhaps preserving our image. A simple example of this is when you are introduced to several people at a party and often forget their names almost immediately, because in a sense you are too caught up with how you are presenting yourself to listen fully — or maybe caught up in the act of listening. Tension often comes from listening too intently. Or another example, when you ask the way somewhere, how often do you forget the directions, simply because you are not relaxed enough to receive them? These are simple examples, but serve to show that we often do not listen as well as we think. And when you are in a situation where you are nervous or slightly on edge, this happens more acutely. Almost the most important thing about it is this; we learn by listening, we learn about other people by listening to what they have to say and how they say it, it is the only way you can observe people and get to know them, and you miss so much if you do not. You also help to put people at ease if they feel you are interested and listening — the genuine desire to listen is perhaps the most important part of establishing good relations.

Along the same lines it is necessary, I think, to realize the value of silence, and not to be afraid of it — there needs to be space between words, for it gives us time to receive and think, and to perceive. It makes us aware of our own inner quiet from which we can receive our strength, and also draws people to you. To listen well, and to recognize the need for silence, requires us to be relaxed within ourselves.

Through the exercises you will open up the possibilities of your voice, so that it will serve you in the way you want it to. You will have to rely on your own judgment — listen to criticism and be open to it for that is how you learn what is reaching other people, but in the end it is your own judgment that is important. I think we know when criticism is valid or not — we must also remember that criticism is a subjective thing, governed by what the listener wants you to be like, but something inside us knows what is valid, and we reject what is not. Very often it is the criticism that hurts a bit which is right, but if you look at if fair and square, it is nothing that cannot be adjusted. It is so often the small adjustments that make the difference.

Ultimately it is what you say that matters, because your voice can only be as interesting as what you have to say. In all good speakers to whom we enjoy listening it is really their attitude to life that interests us, and their commitment to what they are saying — we need not necessarily agree with what they are saying — it is the kind of singleness of purpose which we sense in them that makes them compelling. It is their ability to respond to the situation of the moment immediately, not by covering up anything, or by putting on a mask of any sort, but by being immediately and straightforwardly themselves. In our own way we can all be like that. We exercise the voice so that it can respond to the moment and not let us down or hold us back, but what really matters is that we reveal ourselves, for each of us has something to say which is different and, so, interesting. We must try to rid ourselves of feelings of inadequacy, which usually come from false values anyway, and believe that it is enough to be ourselves — you may alter and improve, but for the moment it is a matter of accepting and believing in yourself.

About the exercises.

With all the exercises, whether it be the ones for relaxation and breathing, for clarity of diction, or for vocal flexibility, each person will take them in his own time, for some people are more ready for them than others. It does not matter how slow you are as long as you become aware of each stage, it is the awareness of the muscles that is important, for it is on that awareness that you can build.

It is not always easy to do voice exercises on your own, because you tend to worry about whether you are doing them correctly or not, and that in itself makes for some tension. I think the exercises in the book are clear, so that if you follow them you need not worry about whether you are doing them right, for really you cannot go wrong with them. To begin with work through the exercises slowly, so that you understand the progression that is there — obviously you will not be able to go through all of them each time. For example, the relaxation and breathing exercises done on the floor take a good deal more time than when you do them sitting or standing, so it may not be possible to do these exercises every time you practise, but if you understand the principle to begin with, then you will understand the other exercises. It is much better to limit yourself to a practicable time each day — like half an hour — and stick to it, than to feel you ought to do an hour, and then not do them because you have not that much time to spare. A short concentrated time is better than a longer time which is perhaps not so well channelled.

Although everyone is at different stages and has varying needs, I think everyone basically requires something from each section, simply because the exercises are so interrelated. As the exercises become easier, so the process becomes quicker and you can be more selective as to what is useful to you and how to achieve what you want.

I do think the exercises work on different levels — on one level they help to open up the voice, and on another they help you to be more relaxed and more confident. Anyway you will see.

6
Relaxation and Breathing

Let us go back to the analogy of the violin for a moment, so that we are quite clear about the reasons for the exercises.

We saw that the breath acted as the violin bow, in that it strikes the vocal cords which act as the strings and vibrate making the initial sound, and that that sound is then resonated in the cavities of the chest, neck and head, as the violin note is resonated in the box of the violin. Thus:

i) we have to make sure we get a good supply of breath
ii) we have to see that the initial sound it makes is good
iii) we have to make sure we get as good use of the resonators as possible

First let us look and see where the breath comes from. If you look at the illustration below, it is clear that there is more room in the bottom half of the chest, therefore more room for breath. In fact the top six pairs of ribs are attached firmly back and front — at the back to the spine, and in the front to the breast-bone or sternum — so that if you take breath into the upper part of the chest the whole rib cage has to move, there is not much room for air, so you get a relatively small amount of air for a large amount of effort. Breathing in the upper chest also makes for a lot of tension in the neck and shoulders. It is therefore to be discouraged. Unfortunately, a lot of athletic training concentrates on this area for breath supply, as it enables you to take quick, short breaths, so that if you have had this sort of training — or in fact any training that has concentrated on the muscular development of the chest and shoulders — you will find it a long process to break this kind of breathing habit which, however, is bad for vocal development. You will see there is considerable room for movement in the bottom half of the chest, partly because the chest is wider there, and partly because the ribs are attached only to the spine at the back. They are attached to each other in front by means of muscle, so that when you breathe in the muscles between the ribs contract and draw them together, so that they swing upwards and outwards. The bottom two pairs are unattached in front — they are what we call floating. If you breathe in the bottom part of your chest you get more breath for less effort, so that is where we concentrate the exercises.

The action of the diaphragm also enlarges the chest and makes room for more air. The diaphragm is a dome-shaped sheet of muscle placed so that it is like the floor of the chest – it is attached to the ribs at the edge so that as they swing out the diaphragm is drawn out and flattened, enlarging the chest downwards. By exercise we can make the diaphragm descend lower and so draw air more deeply into the lungs – this is very important.

So it is the diaphragm and the muscles between the lower ribs that we want to exercise and become aware of, to give us a solid amount of air to give us solid sound. To begin with, in the exercises, you will use more air than you need, ultimately it is not the amount of air you use but the way you use it to make sound that matters.

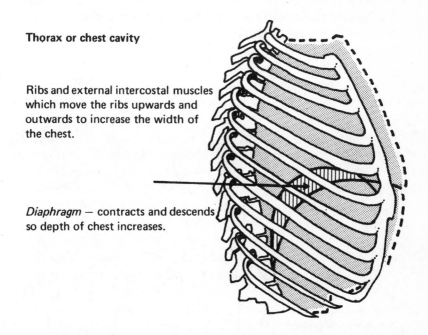

Thorax or chest cavity

Ribs and external intercostal muscles which move the ribs upwards and outwards to increase the width of the chest.

Diaphragm – contracts and descends so depth of chest increases.

Secondly, the breath makes the initial sound by making the vocal cords vibrate. I want to make it clear that the vocal cords come together – or approximate – only when you are going to make sound, or vocalize – when you are breathing normally they are not together and the breath passes through freely. Just as with the violin you can hit the strings too hard, or not hard enough, so with the breath, if you let too much air come through the resulting sound is breathy, or if you use too little the sound is mean. But the vocal cords are not under your direct control, that is to say you cannot feel them separately, except when you misuse them. Sometimes we force the sound out before the breath is ready and so the sound is jerky — that is to say the vocal cords come together first and then we strike them too hard with the breath and get what is called glottal attack or a glottal shock. You can feel this if you say any word beginning with a vowel by hitting it very hard on the vowel sound — say, for instance, the word 'ace' — you can hit it so hard on the initial attack that it jerks out and you can feel something straining in the throat. It is not then a clean smooth attack and can cause fatigue and strain in the voice for the energy should never be in the throat. If the attack is very jerky it can cause permanent damage.

Thirdly, we depend on the resonating spaces to take that initial sound and reinforce it with their own vibrations to give it the specific quality which makes it our voice. We rely on the resonating spaces for the quality of sound we produce — and whether we use the full potential of this resonance depends on our posture and relaxation.

For instance, if your back slumps badly, the ribs will not be free to move as freely as they might. Just for a moment consciously put yourself in a really bad position. First, bend slightly forward at the base of your spine — you will find that you immediately arch backwards from the waist giving yourself a hollow back — you have to do

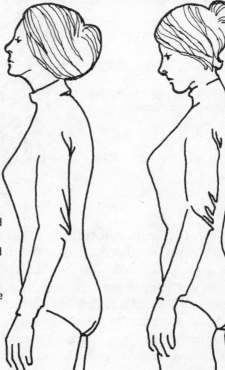

Posture
The left-hand diagram shows how a downward curve of the shoulders pushes the chin out and constricts the neck. The right-hand diagram shows the neck in a free position.

this to maintain your balance. Now, if you try to breathe deeply, you will find that the bottom ribs can hardly move, and they certainly cannot open up round the back which is absolutely vital to the solidity of the tone and your own confidence in being able to sit back on the voice. Now the base of the back can be in a good position, but if you slump your shoulders forward you will find you immediately have to pull the head back to compensate for balance and to keep your head in a normal position. When you pull your head back your neck becomes tense and the potential space there is restricted so that you will get little resonance from the neck.

So you see, one curve in the spine inevitably leads to another, to maintain balance. And one tension leads to another — tension in the small of the back leads to tension in the shoulders — tension in the back of the neck makes the whole neck tense, and constricts the area of the larynx, where the vocal cords are, and the area of the pharynx, just above, where so much good resonance can take place. Tension in the neck also leads to tension in the jaw — thus affecting your freedom in speaking. Try all these tensions out for yourself, then you will be clear about their effect — of course they are exaggerated, but we all get them to some extent or another.

Thus, we see how important good posture is. We also see how totally interdependent breathing and relaxation are and how vital it is to feel the action of each set of muscles separately.

Now for the exercises. We will start on the floor, for that way it is easier to feel the body as a whole, without the tension of having to keep upright. You need a little space so that you do not feel cramped. Above all, take your time.

Exercises

1 Lie on your back on the floor, with your buttocks as flat to the floor as possible — i.e., your seat flat. Take a moment to feel the back spread.

Crook your knees up, a little apart, be aware of them pointing to the ceiling, giving a sensation of being weightless. This should help to get your back flat. However, if there is a hollow in your back do not force it down, just get it as flat as you can, yet comfortable.

Take time to be aware of your back spreading over the floor, and not sinking down into it. Let it spread wide and long.

Let the shoulders spread, try to feel each shoulder joint, not cramped, but easing slightly out of its socket. It helps if you allow the elbows to fall away from the body, with the wrists inwards. Feel the shoulders spread outward from the middle of the back.

Take time to think of your back lengthening along the floor. Be aware of your spine, and try to feel each vertebra slightly easing away from the next so that the back feels long.

Feel this lengthening to the base of the spine — to the tip of the tail.

Take time to be aware of your neck — get the sense that it is lengthening out of your back.

Shake your wrists gently, feel the joints free, let them drop.

Move your elbows, feel the joints free and then let them fall back into place.

Turn the head first to one side and then to the other, feeling the muscles in the back of the neck free, and then back to a central position.

Press the head slightly back into the floor, feel the slight pressure, then release it, noticing the difference. It is the difference between the tension and relaxation of the muscles in the back of the neck that is crucial to feel.

Tense the head slightly forward and down — then free it and feel the difference.

The head should be neither pressed back or forward, but neutral and free.

Take time to allow these sensations of lengthening, widening, and freedom in the different sets of muscles to be separate and clear to yourself.

Go over them again, this time actually telling your muscles what to do:

Back widen

Shoulders free and spread across the floor

Back lengthen down the spine, each vertebra
   separate, feel the length along the floor

Wrists free

Elbows free

Neck free, lengthening out of the back — neither
   pressed back nor forward

The important thing is not to do anything — i.e, not to force your back to lengthen or your arms to spread — they will do this of themselves if you take time to let it happen, for it is extraordinary how muscles will react to orders in this way. Let me give you an example — if I asked you to span an octave on the piano with your fingers and you prepared to do so, but stopped before you actually did, you would feel the muscles and nerve-endings in your fingers react, you would feel a tingling sensation in your finger-tips. You would be conscious of a sensation of your fingers widening without them actually moving — although in fact your fingers would have altered their position slightly. The fingers are obviously much more sensitive than the back and we are more aware of what is happening to them, but it is the same thing that happens to the back — an awareness of the possibility of it widening and lengthening will make it actually do so — it will be fractionally more open, and the sense of release you get from it is remarkable.

In this position, you can be acutely aware of muscular tension and muscular freedom. Try to maintain this awareness of freedom throughout the breathing exercises. If you do tighten up, do not worry, but just keep trying to get back the sensation of freedom. You are bound to tighten quite often at the beginning.

2　Put the backs of the hands quite tightly on the bottom part of the rib cage, where it bulges most, and where we know there is most room for expansion.

a)　Breathe in through the nose, feel the lungs fill with air, and feel the ribs widening out at the back — you should be able to feel them widen on the floor — your hands are there to focus where the movement should be. Sigh out through an open mouth and throat, then push all the air out of the lungs, wait a moment until you feel the need to breathe, then fill in again slowly and sigh out.

Repeat this two or three times only, because it is quite tiring. Breathing in through the nose helps to stimulate the intake. When you breathe out keep the neck as free as possible.

Try to keep the movement to the lower ribs, but do not worry too much if the upper chest moves, this movement will gradually cut out the more you concentrate on widening round the back and lower part of the ribs. But do not feel you have got to fill to such an extent as to get a feeling of tightness in the upper chest.

b)　Breathe in slowly and easily as before — hold a moment to check your shoulders and neck are free — then, counting slowly to yourself, not aloud, breathe out slowly to the count of six, so that you begin to feel the muscles in between the ribs controlling the air. It is important that breathing out should be quite noiseless — if there is any noise in the throat it means that you are constricting something there and are controlling the air in the throat, therefore you are concentrating some energy in the throat, the one place where there should be no tension. Wait before you breathe in again, so that you feel the muscles in between the ribs needing to move and so take in air.

Repeat this exercise several times, increasing the outgoing count to ten — when that is easy, increase it to fifteen. Occasionally try twenty.

To begin with, this exercise should be done for at least five minutes — it is the basic exercise to make you aware of the movement of the ribs and the potential capacity you have. It is lengthy, because, by breathing out so slowly and waiting before you breathe in again, the rib muscles are stimulated to such a degree that you find they will spring out of their own accord, so that you do not have to strain to make them move — you therefore find the energy in those muscles. If you find them difficult to feel at the beginning, apply some pressure with your hands, but not enough to make your shoulders tense.

This exercise opens up the ribs and frees their movement. Now we want to find the movement in the diaphragm, we want to draw the air as deep into the centre as we can.

c) Keep one hand on your ribs, and put the other on the upper part of your stomach. Keeping free in the shoulders and neck, breathe in all the way round, and then give a very small sigh from the stomach where your hand is — like a gentle pant, but not sudden or jerky — then fill in and do it again. You will find it easier to breathe through the mouth.

Repeat this several times — not worrying about what happens to your ribs, they are free to move, and because of the previous exercise they should be nice and open. Just concentrate on little breaths taken in to the deep part of the lungs — the stomach muscles will come out slightly to allow for the move- ment of the diaphragm going down — keep the movement quite specific to where your hand is. Sigh everything out.

d) As with the last exercise, breathe in all the way round, put one hand on your stomach, just below the waist, and give a small sigh out. Breathe in again, feel the air go to where your hand is, and sigh out 'ER', putting a little sound to it on the vowel — it will have a little 'H' in front. Repeat this several times, trying to feel that the air goes in to that point and comes out as sound — you touch the sound off like a drum. It actually starts at that point. So the sound springs from the breath as you release it, and this is what I call 'rooting' the sound. Then relax and be free.

e) Repeat the last exercise, but this time using longer vowels — 'AH', 'AY' and 'I' — holding on to them a little longer and making them firmer. Then sing them quite loudly. Then go back to just touching the vowels off very gently — joining the breath to the sound.

You will now feel that the sound is coming from a deeper place, and you should feel that it sounds fuller. In fact, if the sound is coming from the centre, then the whole chest will contribute to it. Just test this by singing those three vowels, and while you sing them, beat your chest gently so that you feel the vibrations there.

f) Now try to join this up with words — take any piece of poetry or jingle that you know. First make sure your back feels open and free, your neck is free and your shoulders open. Breathe in all the way round, then put your hand on your centre where you feel the movement of the breath going to the diaphragm, give a gentle sigh out to focus on the breath, breathe in again and then speak the lines, feeling the breath joined to the words. Notice any movement of the neck when you start to speak.

It is easier to practise on poetry first — it is more rhythmical for one thing, and because it sounds good it helps you to find good sound. Try it on this seventeenth-century poem of James Shirley, from *Ajax and Ulysses,* written in 1659:

> The glories of our blood and state,
> > Are shadows, not substantial things,/
> There is no armour against fate,
> > Death lays his icy hand on Kings,/
> > > Sceptre and Crown,
> > > Must tumble down,
> And in the dust be equal made/
> With the poor crooked sithe and spade.

To begin with, breathe where I have put the marks, so that you do not have to worry about where to breathe. Take time to breathe, so you feel the breath go right down and the sound come out. If you reach right down to the centre for that sound, then it will be a whole sound, for your whole body will be contributing to it. There will probably be a time-lag between feeling where the breath is coming from, and actually starting the sound from there — this often happens. You can help this by breathing in, then giving a little sigh and being conscious of where it comes from, then breathe in again and speak the lines. The important thing is to feel the sound springing from the centre, or diaphragm.

Now you have worked both the rib muscles and the diaphragm, and you should be feeling much more freedom of sound. It is important that both sets of muscles are working well, for openness of the ribs gives the sound solidity, and starting the sound from the diaphragm helps you to root the sound and focus it. Both are valuable, but do not feel that you have to separate their movements — they relate to each other.

g) Lie still for a moment, affirming the sense of length and width in the back. When you feel ready, roll over slowly onto your side, and stand up, keeping the sense of openness in the back.
When you are standing you should feel very free and rather tall. Take time to notice and remember this feeling.

3 Get a stool or chair without arms, on which you can sit straight but comfortably. Adjust your seat so that your back is as straight as possible without a hollow. Try to recall the sensation you had on the floor when you could feel it long and wide. Give yourself the same orders:
>Back long and wide
>Head lengthening out of the back
>Shoulders free
>Neck free

Head

Drop your head forward, without letting your shoulders slump, and pull it up slowly, feeling the muscles in the back of the head working.
Drop it back and then lift, feeling your head lifting towards the ceiling as you do so.
Drop it to one side, stretch it gently, and then lift.
Drop it to the other side, stretch and lift.
Drop your head forward, roll it round to the side, then right back and to the other side, and forward again. Do this quite slowly, but feeling a very complete head-roll movement.
Repeat this rolling round the other way — be careful not to turn the head as you roll — this is easier.
Hold your head in a normal position again. Tense it very slightly back, as you did on the floor, feeling the tensions in the muscles at the back of the neck, then release it and feel the difference.
Tense your chin slightly down, again feeling the tension in the back neck muscles, release and feel the difference.

62

From this upright-head position nod very gently – really hardly
any movement but just enough to notice the way you can free
the muscles at the back of the neck. This is almost the most
freeing exercise of them all. Just feel the head slightly nodding
on the top of the spine.

Now do a very small head-roll, hardly moving, but as if the head
were on ball-bearings on top of the spine. Then hold it still and
notice how free it feels. Still, but not fixed.

Shoulders

Lift your shoulders very gently, about half an inch or so, then
drop them, but do not let them slump forwards. When you have
dropped them, let them go that extra little bit – they usually
can. Repeat this two or three times, then just feel them sitting
there, and remember that feeling of ease.

These exercises for the neck and shoulders are very gentle and
should be done quietly. Their value is in taking time to be aware of
the muscles and to become familiar with this feeling of freedom, so
that you can remember it and recapture it easily. I think that violent
exercises are not particularly useful, in that they only make you
conscious of the extreme conditions of tension and relaxation – the
kind of passive relaxation which is a negative condition. We want the
feeling of freedom which is alert and ready for movement, and the
more you find it, the more it will stay with you because it will feel
more comfortable. You will find you can do these exercises at odd
moments during the day.

Having found this sense of ease – try to keep it through the
following breathing exercises, which can be done sitting down or
standing up – whichever is most comfortable, though it is probably
best to vary it. Throughout the exercises, keep recalling the sensation
of your back being long and wide, and your head and shoulders free.

4 a) Put your hands up behind your head and let your elbows be
wide – to prevent tension as much as possible just put the tips
of your fingers on your ears to avoid pushing your head forward.
It is a slightly tense position, so you just have to keep as relaxed
as possible, but its great advantage is that it gets the ribs moving
very easily. Breathe in slowly through your nose, trying not to
lift the shoulders, open your mouth and sigh right out – right to
the last bit – and wait. Feel the need to breathe in, and breathe
in again slowly, and out the same way. Then breathe in and
control the outgoing air for six counts – repeat this twice only,
as it is tiring and tension comes quickly.

b) Put the backs of your hands on your ribs, with elbows and wrists as loose as possible; feel the ribs quite firmly with your hands so they have something to resist — it is useful to put one hand on the back sometimes so that you can feel the back ribs opening — then breathe in through your nose for three counts, hold a moment to free the shoulders and neck, then open your mouth and breathe out for ten counts. Wait until you feel the muscles between the ribs needing to move, then breathe in again and repeat. To begin with, when you hold and relax your shoulders, you may find you let the breath out at the same time — this is because the movements are not separate yet and fixing the shoulders is part of breathing deeply. But if you persevere you will soon separate the actions.

This is the basic exercise for opening out the ribs — keep checking that your shoulders and neck are free, that you are not tightening in the throat to control the air, and keep being aware of the muscles between the ribs — for it is these we need to stimulate. When it is easy, increase the count to fifteen, and sometimes to twenty.

When this exercise feels easy, try doing it walking about sometimes — this makes the exercise slightly more difficult, but it also helps to break tension, and starts to bridge the gap between exercise and normal everyday life. The exercises I give you are the basic ones, containing the basic principles, but always feel that you can make up your own variations, according to what is useful to you and what you feel helps you.

c) Now, as you did on the floor, put one hand on the top part of your stomach, just fractionally below the waist, so that you can feel your stomach muscles come out just a little as they give way to make room for the diaphragm. Breathe in all the way round — feeling the ribs opening round the back and sides as well as the breath coming down to the diaphragm — then give a little sigh out from the diaphragm — a gentle pant — fill in again through the mouth, and then sigh again. Repeat this several times so you feel the air being drawn right down to the deep part of the lungs — to the centre.

These breaths can be taken in through the mouth — when we are speaking normally we draw in quick breaths through the mouth — so we are now preparing for a talking rhythm. It is only when you do exercises specifically to make the ribs open that it is good to breathe through the nose.

This exercise is for becoming aware of the movement of the diaphragm. At first, while you are finding awareness, you might feel the movement a little muscular or exaggerated — this is unavoidable. But your aim is that it should be an effortless movement, just an awareness that air is being drawn deep into your centre — in ordinary life one is never conscious of making breathing movements — nor should we be now, but you always have to go through a period of being conscious of the movement while you are extending it.

Do not worry about the ribs in this exercise, they will be mobile and open because of the exercises already done.

Now try vocalising on that diaphragm breath — let it be a very private, easy sound to begin with, for all you are concerned with is joining the breath to the sound. Breathe in, and then touch out on a gentle 'ER' — it will have a little 'H' in front. Then let it gradually become firmer and louder, making sure there is no tension, or small movement forward from the head — everything quite free — just the breath making the sound. Notice particularly that you get a clean start to the vowel, gradually drop the 'H' at the beginning but make sure there is no jerk or glottal stop. You should begin to hear the sound coming from the centre of you. Taking a breath in between each vowel down to the diaphragm, start to spread on the vowel, then use the longer vowels 'AH', 'AY' and 'I'. Speak them first, then sing them on a comfortable note. The sound should be coming from the centre — it should be unforced but firm, and you should feel quite specific as to the place it is starting from. Get the vowels nice and open and feel no push or sense of strain in the throat. The energy is in the breath. Now speak those three vowels quite loudly, concentrating on the breath starting the sound, the extra volume and the extra fullness of sound must come from the breath. Now go back to saying 'ER' quite shortly and privately.

Always keep the feeling of the breath and the sound being as one. When you are doing it quietly, at first you will find the sound breathy — that does not matter because you are discovering the way to do it — but by the end of the exercise it should sound firm.

d) Now try to put this into practice on a piece of text. It will be difficult at first and you may go wrong, but it does not matter — always go on to something which you find difficult — then the simpler things become easy! Prop up a book on the mantelpiece and read what you like — poetry is rather good to start with because you find you can organize the breathing more easily. At this point the aim is not to make the breath last a long time – that will come easily for you never run out of breath in everyday life – the aim now is to become familiar with the complete cycle of breathing that we are after – probably deeper than you are used to and more relaxed.

So, first say to yourself: 'am I standing as well as possible – are my shoulders and neck free', then breathe in and feel the ribs opening round the back. Focus your attention on the diaphragm breath by just sighing out gently from there once or twice, then start to speak. Here is the whole of the poem we started to use, or, if you like, a Shakespeare sonnet:

> The glories of our blood and state,
>   Are shadows, not substantial things,
> There is no armour against fate,
>   Death lays his icy hand on Kings,
>   Sceptre and Crown,
>   Must tumble down,
> And in the dust be equal made,
> With the poor crooked sithe and spade.
>
> Some men with swords may reap the field,
>   And plant fresh laurels where they kill,
> But their strong nerves at last must yield,
>   They tame but one another still;
>   Early or late,
>   They stoop to fate,
> And must give up their murmuring breath,
> When they, pale Captives creep to death.
>
> The Garlands wither on your brow,
>   Then boast no more your mighty deeds,
> Upon Deaths purple Altar now,
>   See where the Victor-victim bleeds,
>   Your heads must come,
>   To the cold Tomb;
> Onely the actions of the just
> Smell sweet, and blossom in their dust.

James Shirley

They that have power to hurt and will do none,
That do not do the thing they most do show,
Who, moving others, are themselves as stone,
Unmoved, cold, and to temptation slow —
They rightly do inherit Heaven's graces,
And husband nature's riches from expense;
They are the lords and owners of their faces,
Others but stewards of their excellence.
The summer's flow'r is to the summer sweet,
Though to itself it only live and die;
But if that flow'r with base infection meet,
The basest weed outbraves his dignity.
 For sweetest things turn sourest by their deeds:
 Lilies that fester smell far worse than weeds.

William Shakespeare

To begin with you will be worrying about everything — your neck — your shoulders — your breathing! But if you do it several times you will begin to feel free and enjoy it — and that is when you start to do good, when you start to hear your voice improving, when you start to hear notes that you have not heard before — there is nothing quite so good for one as a little success. It is the same as singing in the bath — people always say they sing better in the bath. In fact they do — for the acoustics of a bathroom are such that the voice resonates better, so it sounds better — and the fact that it sounds better is encouraging and actually makes you sing better.

So do this until you feel free and begin to enjoy it, then you will experience fuller tone, and once you have experienced this you will not lose it, for you will find it easier to use and it will feel more comfortable.

When you start, the tone will probably be breathy because you will be concentrating on using the breath. Gradually try to make it firmer and fairly loud — that way you can hear and feel what is happening more precisely.

Above all, feel the voice rooted to your centre, and, as it were, feel you are sitting on that sound.

When you feel easy with this, do it walking round, sitting down, stretching up, etc., any kind of movement to make it feel more ordinary and natural.

Now these are the basic exercises for breathing and relaxation — all the other exercises spring from these, because you can adapt them to all specific needs. They should open up an area of awareness and thought about your voice, from which all else springs. Even just thinking about where your voice springs from often makes a great deal of difference. Certainly you should hear a difference almost immediately.

The poems I have given are good, because they sound resonant and it is easier to find fuller tone on something like that. But always end up by saying the piece, or something else, quite conversationally, so that you feel the fuller tone go into your ordinary speaking voice. For, to begin with, you will feel you can only get that kind of sound on a rather low note – this is a misconception, for if the breathing and relaxing are working right the sound will be fuller, whatever pitch you are speaking on.

e) Now try another exercise for releasing sound. You will need plenty of space for this as you are going to swing your arms from one side to the other.

Stand upright with your feet a little apart, and put your arms up to one side, stretch them up, then let them swing right down to the floor letting your trunk swing down with them, and swing them up again to the other side. The really important thing to remember is that when you swing over forward you must let your head and shoulders go completely – feel as much weight as possible when you swing down, so that the swing down impels the movement up to the other side. Do this once to get the idea of the movement.

Now, as you take your hands up to one side, draw breath in and as you swing down let the breath out on the vowel 'AY' speaking it quite loudly, then swing up to the other side and breathe in. Swing down again saying the vowel 'I' – allow the energy of the swing down to impel the vowels out. Do this at an easy pace, several times. Then do the same thing, but singing the vowels out on a comfortable note.

Rest for a moment. Then do the same thing again, but this time speaking the poem two lines to a breath, and swing, really allowing the sound to come out and making sure the neck and shoulders fall forwards completely free.

Immediately you have done this, without taking time to collect yourself – i.e., think! – speak it in a normal standing position You will find that the resulting sound is enormously free.

This is a marvellous exercise for releasing sound, for it catches you unawares, and you can do it on any piece of text that is useful to you, but always end up saying it quite still. What it does is this: because you are moving quite forcefully, you are having to take more breath; because you are moving from the waist the air gets drawn right down to there without you thinking about it, and because you are dropping over so completely, your shoulders and neck are quite free — you cannot hold them or fix them.

It makes you aware of the whole mechanism coming together, and you hear full, vital tone — a valuable experience, for the more you experience this sound, the more readily you will be able to call on it.

The same freeing thing happens if you do star jumps while speaking the text — leap, really pushing your arms up and out, and then speak, standing still. The result in both cases is quite remarkable.

You see, it not only releases you physically, it takes away from that over-concentration which you are almost bound to get when doing voice exercises on your own. Over-concentration is in itself a tensing thing, because you have all the responsibility of doing the exercises and checking yourself while you are doing them. You will find that the movement allows the voice to take on textures that you did not know you had, and releases sound not consciously produced and rhythms which may surprise you. So always feel you can do some part of your exercises moving about — though the releasing will not happen without good solid exercises first.

Sometimes beat your chest when you speak, to encourage the vibrations there.

Whether you use the poems I have given here, or something of your own choice, you are using them as a bridge between doing exercises and speaking normally, so that it does not matter if the phrasing is odd or the meaning not clear. To begin with you will be over-conscious of breath, but that will gradually put itself right, and eventually you will feel that to root the breath and the sound in this way is, in fact, easier and it will become something you want to do normally.

The next step is to try it out on something more demanding, where you are not only going for good sound and good breathing, but where you are also thinking of the sense and have to grapple with it a bit — either telling a story or pursuing an argument. There is a vast choice of material to use. It certainly helps to begin with something rather formal, for if you practise on something out of a neswpaper, it seems absurd and false to open the voice out on it. Therefore it helps at the start to do something which sounds good of itself. I am including here the Chorus in *Henry V,* Act III and a small extract from Book I of *Paradise Lost,* but it can be anything that appeals to you, the proviso being that it requires to be spoken aloud. In both cases I have marked where to breathe, for this is helpful at first, but later, when you feel easy, you can breathe where you like. Rhetorical speeches are good for this purpose — sermons, such as those of Donne or Knox. Any speeches from Shakespeare are excellent, and passages from any of the Shaw plays are good too — the speech of the Devil for instance, in *Man and Superman,* is a great exercise. Also the poems of Shelly, Dylan Thomas or Yeats, and the plays of Marlowe — texts which stretch the voice in some way and are bigger in thought and expression than everyday speech.

Some people object to taking good material and using it for the purpose of exercise. Personally I think the better the material, the more likely you are to get good results from your voice, provided you are aware of the level at which you are using it — also you always learn something from it, and it enriches one's experience.

Take the Shakespeare at its story level. The Chorus is there to set the scene for us — there was no scenery in Shakespeare's theatre, so the words had to do the job for it. It paints a picture of the king setting sail from England with his army, for France, to lay siege to Harfleur. As you become familiar with the text, so the narrative will get clearer — allow yourself to react to the words and the picture they paint. The Milton is good to do — it is the speech of Satan after he was turned out of heaven — because you cannot hurry over it, there is great weight and quantity in the sounds he uses, so take it slowly and feel the breath very steady on it.

You are using both pieces as an extension to your breathing exercises so:

i)   Check that your posture is good

ii)   Check that your shoulders and neck are free

iii)   Take plenty of time to breathe fully before you start — feel the ribs open, get the diaphragm working and feel the sound springing from the centre by sighing out from there and vocalizing on a vowel.

iv)   Feel the throat open

v)   Root the sound, and feel that you are sitting on it

vi)   Be aware of your chest contributing to the sound

vii)   Keep a sense of talking throughout, however loud you get, because this keeps the voice flexible and the range open.

From *HENRY V, ACT III*

Chorus: Thus with imagined wing our swift scene flies,
In motion of no less celerity
Than that of thought./ Suppose that you have seen
The well-appointed King at Hampton pier
Embark his royalty;/ and his brave fleet
With silken streamers the young Phoebus fanning./
Play with your fancies; and in them behold
Upon the hempen tackle ship-boys climbing;/
Hear the shrill whistle which doth order give
To sounds confus'd;/behold the threaden sails,
Borne with th'invisible and creeping wind,
Draw the huge bottoms through the furrowed sea,
Breasting the lofty surge./ O, do but think
You stand upon the rivage and behold
A city on th'inconstant billows dancing;/
For so appears this fleet majestical,
Holding due course to Harfleur./ Follow, follow!
Grapple your minds to sternage of this navy
And leave your England as dead midnight still,
Guarded with grandsires, babies, and old women,
Either past or not arriv'd to pith and puissance;/
For who is he whose chin is but enrich'd
With one appearing hair that will not follow
These cull'd and choice-drawn cavaliers to France?/
Work, work your thoughts, and therein see a siege;/
Behold the ordnance on their carriages,
With fatal mouths gaping on girded Harfleur./
Suppose th'ambassador from the French comes back;/
Tells Harry that the King doth offer him
Katherine his daughter, and with her to dowry
Some petty and unprofitable dukedoms./
The offer likes not; and the nimble gunner
With linstock now the devilish cannon touches,

And down goes all before them./ Still be kind,
And eke out our performance with your mind.

William Shakespeare

When you first do this you will think perhaps that it is rather high-flown poetry, but the more you do it the more you will find that it tells a very particular story and describes a very particular scene. It tells us we have to work our thoughts to imagine a stage filled with sailors and ships and cannon — it is so alive it is like a film camera picking out the shots you should see. The words are colourful — yes — but also accurate. And the freer you get with the technical means — i.e., the breathing and relaxation — the more vividly will you be able to paint the word picture. Go for the sense.

From *PARADISE LOST, BOOK I*

> Is this the Region, this the Soil, the Clime,
> Said then the lost Arch Angel,/this the seat
> That we must change for Heav'n, this mournful gloom
> For that celestial light?/ Be it so, since hee
> Who now is Sovran can dispose and bid
> What shall be right:/ fardest from him is best
> Whom reason hath equald, force hath made supream
> Above his equals./ Farewel happy fields
> Where Joy for ever dwells:/ Hail horrours, hail
> Infernal world, and thou profoundest Hell
> Receive thy new Possessor:/ One who brings
> A mind not to be chang'd by Place or Time./
> The mind is its own place, and in it self
> Can make a Heav'n of Hell, a Hell of Heav'n./
> What matter where, if I be still the same,
> And what I should be, all but less than he
> Whom Thunder hath made greater?/ Here at least
> We shall be free; th'Almighty hath not built
> Here for his envy, will not drive us hence:/
> Here we may reign secure, and in my choyce
> To reign is worth ambition though in Hell:
> Better to reign in Hell, than serve in Heav'n./
> But wherefore let we then our faithful friends,
> Th'associates and copartners of our loss
> Lie thus astonisht on th'oblivious Pool,/
> And call them not to share with us their part
> In this unhappy Mansion, or once more
> With rallied Arms to try what may be yet
> Regaind in Heav'n, or what more lost in Hell?

John Milton

Now you have begun to use the resources of your voice. By opening and widening the ribs – particularly at the back, because there you feel no sense of strain, just a sense of openness – you will make the chest alive to the resonance it can give without any effort – it is gratuitous resonance as it were. And it is this openness of the ribs that gives the tone a kind of solidity, on which you can sit back. I know I use a lot of images like that – 'sitting back on the tone' – but I think they work – one's imagination responds to them. By the diaphragm drawing the breath down to the centre of you, you find a sound which is specific and which has a base – a firmness which, you will find, carries well. It is not woolly tone, but defined and clear. You will find that the sound springs from that centre, so that when you have to project to a large space, you are not having to push the sound out, but are loosing it like an arrow, and by wanting it to reach further, it *will* reach further without a desperate increase of volume and straining for sound. The energy, you will find, is within you. Also, finding the sound in this way does not make it heavy, or 'actorish', or 'well-produced', because all you are using is yourself, your own skeletal structure, so it can only be more particular to you – and, in fact, it opens out the upper register more, so you can use more notes yet still feel the voice has quality. It makes good sense – I think! To be able to open the sound out, yet keep yourself free, makes you able to use all the hollow spaces in the neck and at the back of the tongue to amplify the sound, and give it its full quality. So when you are working on one of these rather large, heightened pieces of text, allow the voice to spread, and use as much range as you can, for it is only by doing this that you will find out what you have got.

Now to start relating this to your particular needs. Obviously, if your aim is simply to make your voice freer and fuller in the context of ordinary conversation and social ease, then you will not want a great deal of power, but you will want to call on the deeper notes of the voice, you will want the sense of freedom I have described, and you will want to centre your voice, for that way it contains its own quiet authority. But if you do a lot of speaking in public – preaching teaching etc., then you will want to know more about increasing volume without losing quality, and increasing the textural richness and range.

Size without Tension

Nowadays most speakers who have to face a large audience have the use of microphones. To use a microphone well has more to do with sharpness of diction than anything else. But there are quite a number of situations, particularly in classrooms or lecture halls, where there is a sizeable area to fill without any mechanical aid. And in any case it is good to know how to increase the size of your voice.

I think the first thing you tend to do, when faced with a large audience, is to 'speak up'. This is probably a hangover from childhood, and is an unfortunate phrase because it immediately makes you think of talking at a higher pitch, and also has the implication that a high pitch carries better, which is not necessarily true. Immediately you do go up in pitch, you get just a little tight in the neck, the voice loses its natural talking inflections and gets hard, and you start talking *at* your audience and not *to* them. So you stop drawing your audience, and you alienate them instead – for the sound comes out at the same pressure and assaults the ear – you lose the attention of your audience.

Here are some variations on the basic exercises to help: – by the way, it is good to have a piece of text learnt, so that you can play around with it.

a) Lie on the floor and loosen up, get the ribs and diaphragm working freely, and particularly concentrate on keeping the neck and shoulders free. Speak some lines of text that you know – like the Shakespeare – begin quietly, and gradually increase the volume as you go on, but take care that you keep it keyed to the same pitch. That is to say, keep quite conversational and use plenty of inflection, but always come down and resolve it to the same base note.

b) Stand up, and start speaking the text with your hands behind your head to get the ribs open. As you go on gradually bring the arms down.

c) Sing part of your text quite loudly on one note, making the breath last out to the end of the phrase to sustain the phrases, then speak some of it, conscious of the breath supporting the sound.

d) Shout two or three lines of text, taking care not to tense your neck, then speak the rest, always feeling the extra energy from the centre.

e) Jog very heavily round the room, or on one spot, feeling a great weight as you jog, and speak while you are doing this, gradually increasing the volume without letting the pitch go up.

As with everything to do with the voice, your own attitude is as important as your technical means. When you look at a large space and a sea of faces, you tend to go at the lot, and be general, but you are not talking to a lot of people, you are talking to a number of individuals, and you assume they want to listen. All you have to do, is mentally — I prefer spiritually — reach out to them and share what you have to share. If you think like that, the voice will immediately spring.

Increase of texture and weight of sound.

Actually this has to do with finding a more musical tone, but I do not mean this in a false way, it is just that some people have particularly dry voices and need to work extra hard on getting resonance from the chest. Try these:

a) Do plenty of work on the floor, speaking the text, checking regularly to see there is no tension in the neck. Use the floor as a sounding board and feel the vibrations of the chest.

b) Lie on the floor on your front, feeling spread, and with your head turned to one side. Hum in this position, and feel the vibrations on the floor — also speak and sing some text.

c) Standing, do the same as the last exercise, but humming and speaking into a corner, so that the walls bounce back some of your sound. If you have a piano, speak right down into the body of it, where the strings are, with the sustaining pedal on. You will hear vibrations coming back at you, which will help you to increase your own.

d) Sing a piece of text like an operatic recitative, making up your own tune as you go along. Then speak it normally.

Breathiness.

This can be general breathy tone, or breathy attack at the beginning of phrases, letting all your air out at the beginning and then tailing away at the end. All the singing exercises we have done are particularly useful for this. But also:

a) Exercise a lot with your hands behind your head — though not keeping them there long enough to be tense,

b) It is valuable, sometimes, to reverse the timing of the rib exercises, so that you breathe in for a long count of ten to fifteen, and out for a short count of three.

c) Breathe in as fully as you can, focus on your diaphragm breath, and hum out smoothly on 'M' for six, then eight, then ten counts, increasing the count out as it becomes easy.

d) Repeat the last exercise, but focus the hum on an object, and let the 'M' be like a line coming out of your mouth to attach itself to that object. Do the same with the vowels 'OO', 'OH', 'AH', 'AY' and 'I'.

Repeat the last exercise, always reaching to your centre for the sound, but focussing on objects at different distances, first fairly near, then further away — it can be an object outside the window. The important thing is to make the sound go further, not by getting louder, but by increasing the density of the sound. This also helps with projecting your voice. Always be quite precise about the object on which you are focussing.

If the attack is breathy and you tail away at the ends:

e) Go through a text making the phrases you tackle unnaturally long, then go through it normally.

f) Experiment by intentionally stressing and elongating the last word of a phrase — this is good because it opens up the possibilities of meaning on the last word. This is a particularly limiting fault in that the rhythm of your phrases becomes repetitive and lacks energy and a drive to follow through to something else.

Overbalance of head resonance.

Some people have a lot of resonance and vibration in the head — the nose, sinuses and bones of the face. This is not a bad thing in itself, for it gives the tone a kind of brilliance, but it is bad if it overbalances the chest notes, because it gets a metallic quality — it is as if the tone had a skin on it, and lacks warmth and flexibility. For, however much you alter the pitch and inflection of the voice, if the head resonance is so dominant, it will not appear to have any flexibility. It is always caused by some tension in the throat — the soft palate to be precise — which then cuts off any of the undertones that you might have and negates the openness of the breath.

You cannot feel the soft palate separately as you can feel the lips for instance, but by exercising it with the back of the tongue and saying 'g' and 'k' you can feel its action.

So to get a feeling of freedom in the palate try this:

Say 'ge ge ge' so that you become aware of the soft palate coming down to meet the back of the tongue. Do the same with 'ke ke ke'.

Then press the back of the tongue very hard against the palate, so that the sets of muscles are consciously tense, and say 'ge', using quite a bit of pressure. Be conscious of that tension.

Now, consciously drop the jaw, allow the back of the palate to drop, feel the back of the tongue relaxed, and say 'ge' again — firmly but relaxed.

Let the jaw drop open and say 'AH', and notice the freedom at the back of the tongue, and the space that there is there for resonance.

I think this to be one of the most important exercises in the book, because so much good tone is negated by a small amount of tension in this one spot, for it is here where so much tension is centred.

So the drill is this:

'ge ge ge'   —   tight
'ge ge ge'   —   relaxed
drop open and say 'AH'

Then breathe in and say a few lines of text, trying to maintain that sense of openness.

Glottal attack.

If your attack is very jerky, most of it will get ironed out by the exercises already given. But it is good to sing out on different vowel sounds, first preceding them with 'H', and then thinking the 'H' but not saying it. Do the same speaking the vowels. Take time over this, for it is a matter of sensing the precise co-ordination of the breath with the vowel.

There are enough exercises here to keep you busy — vary them as it helps you. Find good stuff to speak that you can enjoy. As you progress you will find that what is in the text becomes more important than the exercise. This is as it should be, because the voice will always be at its best when your imagination, or interest in what you are saying, takes over and makes the voice do what it wants.

There are two postscripts to this chapter. First is a very important point about vocal fatigue. If you feel that you get excessive vocal fatigue, and only you can tell this, and if there is any continuing pain or soreness in the throat that worries you, then you should see a doctor. If it is temporary he will give you something to ease it, but he will know if you should see a laryngologist. Sometimes tension over a long period, or too much attack on the vocal cords can cause roughness on them and eventually you get nodes, which are like small corns, on them. This can be caused by having to speak very loudly when you have had a sore throat and are not quite over the infection. It is not a common condition, but continued strain there should be investigated.

Secondly, about smoking — people are always asking me if it harms the voice. I think it has little effect if you smoke moderately — say, ten a day — but if you smoke heavily it obviously causes a certain amount of congestion, so that your lungs do not fill properly, and it causes a good deal of catarrh, which constricts the throat and, in the end, limits considerably the range of notes you can use.

7
Speech

We know that we do not necessarily want to iron out any dialect or accented speech, but we know we do want to make the speech clear, firm and vital. Clarity comes from having firm clear consonants, and reasonably open, unclipped vowels, and this we can achieve by exercising the muscles involved. What is good about these exercises is that you can feel the benefit very quickly – more so than with relaxation and breathing.

The exercises not only make the speech clearer, at the same time they help you to place the tone forward so that it carries better. It is the sharpness of the consonant that makes the word impinge at a distance, so you are at the same time taking the strain off projection and reaching a large space – particularly if that space is over-resonant as most churches are, for instance. For projection is only in part to do with volume, it is more to do with sending out the word and the energy that you find in the word.

First of all we will define a consonant and a vowel, and then we will see what sets of muscles we use to make them.

A Consonant

This is a sound in which the passage of air or sound is stopped, or partially stopped, by some part of the mouth, so that consonants fall into two groups – plosive and continuant. You will notice that the plosives – k, g, t, d, p, b, ch, dj – all have the passage of sound stopped for a split second by either the lips or the tongue, so that it is held before it is released, and it is not until the muscles release the air that we actually hear the sound. It is important that we know what happens, because it is in the timing of the action that clarity can be lost. Take 'p' or 'b', for example. In both cases the muscles press the lips together to stop the air coming out, they hold the sound for a moment, and when the lip muscles are released, the 'p' and 'b' explode out. Just do it once for yourself, exaggerating the pressure and movement – press the lips hard together – hold a moment – then let the 'p' sound explode out like a cork popping. Do the same with 'b'. The same thing happens with 't' and 'd' – the tongue-tip is pressed against the ridge behind the teeth and held for a moment before being released. With 'k' and 'g', as we have already seen, it is the contact between the back of the tongue and the soft palate that forms the consonant.

With 'ch' and 'dj' it is the closing of the jaw and the tongue pressed against the teeth and hard palate that makes the stoppage. In all these cases, sound or air is stopped for a fraction of a second and when it is released we then hear the consonant. You will also notice that these plosive consonants fall into pairs, so that one of each pair is what we call 'voiced' — that is to say the vocal cords come together when you say it and so it is sounded or vibrated. The other one of the pair is what we call 'breathed' — it comes out on the breath. Just say each of these pairs quietly to yourself and see the difference;

p	—	b
t	—	d
k	—	g
ch	—	dj	(this is the hard 'g' sound, as in badge, as opposed to the soft 'g' as in *rouge,* or the middle sound in measure)

In the first column it is breath that explodes out and we only hear vocalized sound when we put a vowel on the end as in 'pie', 'tie', 'kite', 'child'. The second column of consonants is vocalized and it is sound that explodes outwards. Say the second column again slowly, this time holding on to the consonants before you let the sound out, and you should feel the different sets of muscles involved, tingling with the vibrations that could be made. It is the possible vibrations on these consonants that are important to us, for if you make them firmly they will contain vibration or resonance, and so add extra resonance to your own sound. This is vitally important. Now, put one hand about a couple of inches in front of your mouth and say the first column of consonants — you will notice that with each of them quite a bit of air explodes out, which you can feel on your hand. This is most important, because it is that 'aspiration', as we call it, that makes those particular consonants carry and cut up the vowels sharply, so that we can hear each word clearly. The breath should not come out while you are closing the consonant — with 't', for instance, you can say 't' and let some air out while the tongue tip is against the ridge at the back of the teeth — this makes for a messy 't', we associate it with Cockney speech, and it means that you are not making the muscular closure firmly enough — the muscles of the tip of the tongue are being flabby. An Irish 't', on the other hand, lets a lot of air out before the closure and we get a lot of aspiration — in some Irish accents there is really hardly any closure at all, just a slightly pressured aspiration at that position. Also, even though 'b' and 'd' are voiced consonants, a little air comes out when you explode them, though less than with the breathed ones. Say them over again slowly, noticing the difference. It is important that you feel and hear this, for aspiration is part of English speech — it gives it its edge or sharpness, and time has to be allowed for it. In French speech, for instance, there is less aspiration — their 't' may consequently sound almost like a 'd' — as in *tête.*

Time taken over consonants is important. Quite often speech is unclear, not because the muscular movement is not right, simply that not enough time is allowed for the consonant to make its impact. This is particularly true when speaking in a large space with a fair amount of volume — the further you want the voice to carry, the more time you need to give the consonants. The louder you speak, the sharper the consonants have to be to break up the vowels — for that is in fact what they do — they divide up the vowel sounds to make the syllable units. This is really a rule that you can remember.

Now we come to the continuant consonants, which can also be both breathed and voiced. Their passage of air or sound is only partially stopped by the tongue or lips, so that it is possible to go on saying them for as long as your breath lasts out — in other words, they are continuant!

Here they are:

NG – made with the back of the tongue and the soft palate, in the same place as 'k' and 'g'. In English, it is only used at the end of words.

M – made by the lips being pressed together, as with 'p' and 'b'

N – made by the tongue tip pressing against the ridge at the back of the teeth, as with 't' and 'd'

How does the sound escape in these three sounds? In fact the soft palate comes down and allows the sound to escape through the nose. They are all voiced sounds. Put your hand just under your nose, and feel the air coming down while you make the sound.

So, they are not only continuant, they are what we call nasal consonants, and the sound is resonated in the nose, which, if used well, adds good resonance to the voice. When you have an over-nasal sound, it simply means that you are letting the nasal resonance overlap into the vowel sound, so that the whole voice sounds nasal.

Diagrams of the position of the nasal consonants with their plosive consonant positions —

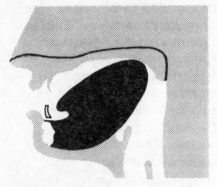

For 'K' and 'G' the back of the tongue articulates with the uvula, which is up, leaving no space for the sound to pass up into the nose.

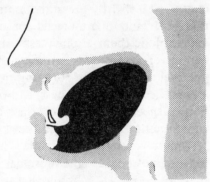

For 'NG' the uvula is lowered so that the sound can pass into the nasal cavity.

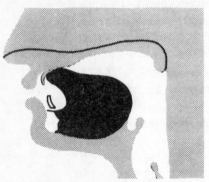

For 'T' and 'D', the tip of the tongue is up against the teeth ridge and the uvula is raised.

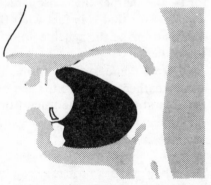

For 'N' the tip of the tongue is pressed against the teeth ridge, but the uvula is lowered to allow the sound to pass out through the nose.

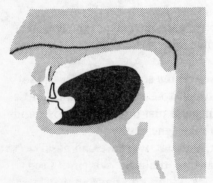

For 'P' and 'B' the lips are pressed together and the uvula is raised.

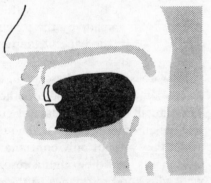

For 'M' the lips are pressed together, but the uvula is lowered to allow the sound to pass into the nose.

The other continuant consonants are these:

L   — made by placing the tip of the tongue against the ridge behind the teeth, stopping the sound there, but with the sides of the tongue lowered, allowing the sound to continue out. In English this consonant is always voiced, but Welsh speech has a breathed 'l', as at the beginning of Llandudno.

R   — again made with the front of the tongue, but this time with it curved up and slightly back, so that it is almost in contact with the curve of the hard palate — enough to give it friction and vibration, but not enough to stop the sound. There is also the rolled 'R', or the one-tap 'R', which is made by a very rapid bouncing of the tongue-tip against the teeth ridge. This is what we recognise as a Scottish 'R'. Newcastle speech has a different variety, which is akin to the French 'R', where it is the back of the tongue coming in close proximity to the back of the palate which makes the friction and so the sound.

It is always a voiced sound.

The rest of the continuant consonants go in pairs — voiced and breathed. They are:

s - z   — made with the jaw more or less closed and the tip of the tongue pressed against the teeth — the sound escapes down the channel in the centre of the tongue and through the interstices of the teeth. The exact position of the tongue is variable.

f - v   — these are made with the top teeth biting against the lower lip — not too hard — so that there is friction between the teeth and the lip as the breath escapes.

th - th   — the first one as in 'thin', and the second as in 'this' — the same sound, one breathed and the other voiced. These are made with the tongue tip slightly through the teeth, and friction is created between the teeth and the tongue tip as the sound comes out.

With these last six consonants it is the amount of friction that you allow to come out that makes them carry. It is possible to make them with too much pressure, almost stopping the sound so they become like plosive consonants — try this for yourself and you will find that the sound does not carry. When speech lacks clarity it is very often because you are not letting enough breath or vibration out on these sounds — it is the friction caused by the pressure of the muscles that make them carry. Consequently they are very good to practise on — the breathed ones help you to be aware of the placing of the tone forward in the mouth. The voiced ones help you to be aware of the possibility of the vibration, and therefore resonance, that the tongue and lips can contribute to the whole sound. This resonance from the muscles themselves gives a whole new dimension to the sound, as you will see when you start the exercises.

These are all the consonants, and you will now have found all the parts of the mouth that make the sounds. Just to be quite clear they are:

The tongue tip
The back of the tongue
The lips
The back of the palate, or soft palate, which can move up
   and down
The hard palate, which does not move
The teeth ridge, just behind the teeth
The jaw, which is open to varying degrees.

Parts of the mouth

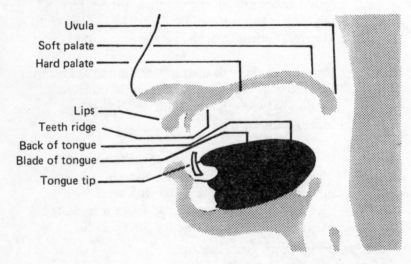

Uvula
Soft palate
Hard palate

Lips
Teeth ridge
Back of tongue
Blade of tongue
Tongue tip

Now for the Vowels

A vowel is always voiced, and of course is always continuant. The jaw has to be open, so the vowel always has a free passage of sound through the mouth, but it is shaped in different ways — it is the shape of the lips which defines the lip vowels, and the position of the tongue which defines the tongue vowels. There are twelve pure vowels in English speech — that is to say the shape does not alter while you say them. There are seven diphthongal sounds — vowels made with two sounds glided together and said in the same space of time as one vowel. And there are two triphthongal sounds, where you have three sounds glided together and said as one vowel.

The following are the vowel sounds shaped by the lips, you will see that the shape of the lips varies from being very closed to open:

OO — as in 'lose'
oo — as in 'look'
AW — as in 'law'
o — as in 'lot'
AH — as in 'lark' (for this the lips are quite open, there is really no shaping).

You will see that I have put some in capital letters. These are intrinsically longer sounds than the others — though the length of long or short vowels varies, as we shall see, according to the consonants that follow.

The tongue vowels are as follows — I start with 'AH' again, because the tongue is flat:

AH — as in 'large'
u — as in 'luck'
ER — as in 'learn'
er — as at the end of 'father' (a very short vowel — almost a neutral one, for we often use it in place of other vowels in quick speech)
a — as in 'lad'
e — as in 'let'
i — as in 'link'
EE — as in 'leave'

Say these vowels through slowly, noticing what happens to your tongue. You will find that from the flat position of 'AH', the front part of the tongue gradually arches upward, so that 'EE' is very arched in the front of the mouth. To feel this properly you have to consciously keep the tip of the tongue down behind the front teeth, which of course is not normally done in speech — it is always moving from or to a consonant.

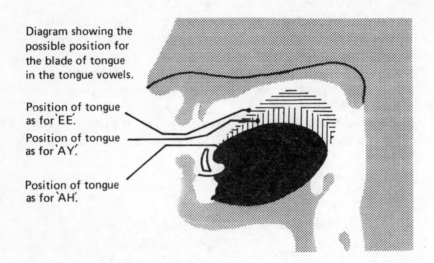

Diagram showing the possible position for the blade of tongue in the tongue vowels.

Position of tongue as for 'EE'.

Position of tongue as for 'AY'.

Position of tongue as for 'AH'.

The diphthongal vowels are as follows: the lip sounds first
  OH — as in 'go' (you start from a neutral position of the lips, and round it towards 'oo')
  OW — as in 'house' (which starts roughly at 'u' and rounds towards 'oo')
  OI — as in 'boy' (which starts with the lip sound 'AW' and goes towards the tongue sound 'i')

The tongue sounds:
  AY — as in 'hay' (which starts at 'e' and goes towards 'i')
  I   — as in 'sky' (which starts roughly at 'u' and goes towards 'i')
  AIR — as in 'hair' (which starts with a very open 'e' sound and goes towards 'er')
  EER — as in 'ear' (which starts with a close 'i' sound and goes towards 'er')

The two triphthongs are simply 'IRE', which is 'I' with 'er' as in 'hire' or 'choir'
and 'OUR' which is 'OW' with 'er' as in 'hour' or 'flour'

With the diphthongs, in each case I have said they go towards the second sound — the weight is always on the first part of the sound and actually should not dwell on the second, though in certain speech it does. In Cockney speech, for instance, in 'AY' and 'I' the second part of the sound gets elongated so that the vowels have a strong 'EE' quality, and so sound closed.

It is important to realize that it is the vowel that carries the weight of the tone, so that if the vowel is breathy, the tone will be breathy. If the vowel is hard and thin, the tone will be mean. If the vowel is nasal, the tone will be nasal. And the jaw plays an important part in this, for if the jaw is tight and closed, the vowel cannot be open and free, so the tone will be tight.

Also you will see that I have given you the vowels in isolation — in their pure form as it were — and of course in quick speech they can never be quite as well formed as that, and very often we substitute a neutral vowel for another one — that is quite right, otherwise the speech would be too formal. The important thing is to be able to feel the vowels in their complete state, then you will know how much variation you are giving them. It is, for instance, possible to make the following progression of vowel sounds with an almost closed jaw, and with very little movement of the tongue — the vowels will still be recognizable. Try it, first with the vowels on their own, and then with words:

AH — u — ER — a — e — AY — i — EE
bark — but — bird — bad — bed — bake — bit — beat

You will discover that all the movement is going on in the back of the tongue and it is quite effortful to do it. Yet a lot of speech is like that, — taking place at the back of the mouth, with no clear definition and very clamped sound. Try the same progressions again, trying to keep the jaw loose and slightly exaggerating the opening of the vowels. Obviously that will be too much also, but you can then feel something happening, an aliveness in the front of the mouth, and a feeling that the vowels want to come out — they are being sent out. So we clearly want speech that is free, but not noticeably open.

There is all the difference in the world between speech made with little or no muscular movement because the muscles are stiff and immobile, and speech made with little apparent muscular movement, but with the muscles free and alive and having energy. For it is the muscles in the tongue, lips and palate which have energy and which can impel the words out of themselves without effort.

You will see that the movements involved in making speech are comparatively small and take place within a small area. The smallest variation of placing and movement can make an enormous difference. Because the movements take place within such a restricted area, it is difficult to isolate the awareness of the muscles and feel their movement separately. To work the muscles separately you have to have the jaw open, about half an inch, and it is almost impossible to stop it closing. I think it is invaluable to start the exercises by putting something between your teeth to keep the jaw open and steady. The best

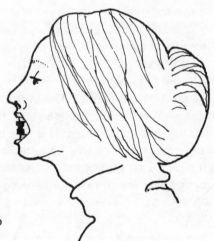

How to place the bone-prop
in the mouth.

thing is a bone-prop, which is specially made to hold the mouth open. These can be bought from John Bell & Croyden of 50 Wigmore Street, London – a large chemist's. It is a plastic prop, about the thickness of a pencil, which has a groove at each end to fit onto the teeth, so that it does not slip. You put it in at the front of the mouth. In fact, most people can find a way of making something similar – with the top part of a plastic pen, a piece of cork, or a wooden meat skewer – try to make a groove for the teeth to fit into, otherwise, with pressure from the jaw, it is apt to jump out and can hurt the gums. It should not be too thick or it will get in the way of the tongue movement. Also, and this is vitally important, it should not be too long – for most people half an inch or three-quarters of an inch is quite long enough. Some people may find even a half inch too long. You will have to rely solely on your common sense for this. It should be wide enough to make the movement of the lips and tongue difficult, but not impossible. If you find it sets up a great deal of tension in the jaw, then do not use one — instead do the exercises in front of a mirror, so that you see how much you are closing the jaw and can adjust accordingly. Also, some people find that it makes them feel sick, if this is so then obviously do not use one. Also, some people find that their teeth are set in such a way that it makes it too difficult to use one — either the top jaw overlaps too much, or the teeth are set at an angle — sometimes the solution is to use a very small prop, but to put it in at the side of the mouth. Otherwise, as I say, keep checking in a mirror, or put a finger on each side of the mouth, pressing lightly to keep the jaw open. However, the bone-prop is by far the best to use, as a few minutes with it in makes the muscles so alive that when you take it out you will be surprised at the firmness and clarity of the speech, however, do use it with discretion and be careful not to swallow it accidentally — it has been done!

Using a prop is simply a way to get the muscles moving — do not feel that all that movement is the norm — good speech should never be noticeable — only alive!

One more thing before we begin the exercises, always check the freedom of the neck before you start, and at intervals during the exercise. The desire to make the consonants firm very often makes you push with the head — this is a very common fault — but our aim is to find the energy in the muscles that are making the sound, so any extra movement is waste — it also constricts the sound.

Exercises

1 *Jaw* Drop it open gently — find the most open position without tension — hopefully this will be about the width of two fingers. Open and close it gently several times to feel it loose. If it does not open easily, then you will have to work at it gently over a fairly long period, loosening it at odd times through the day so that it gradually loosens up. Chewing movements help this.

2 *Tip of the tongue* Put the prop in between the front teeth.
a) Place the tongue tip against the teeth ridge, though not touching the teeth — there should be about an eighth of an inch of the flat of the tongue against the ridge — keep the tongue there for a moment to feel its position, then release it and say 'lah'.
   Feel the back of the tongue free and relaxed, and the throat open, let the 'l' spring easily into the open vowel 'AH'. Let the tongue tip come to rest against the bottom teeth. The tension should be specific to the tongue tip, and the movement should not be jerky, but should spring the vowel out — so that it is firm but

light.

Keeping that movement complete – i.e., the tongue coming down to the bottom teeth and the vowel really open, exercise rhythmically thus:

lah	lah	lah	lah
lala	lala	lala	lala
lalala	lalala	lalala	lalala

The rhythm should be precise and the movement accurate – do not slur as you increase the number of syllables.

When you have done it several times with the prop in, repeat with the prop out, keeping the movement firm and effortless – it should feel good.

b) Prop in again. With the tongue tip pressed firmly against the teeth ridge and the sides up against the gums say 'tah'. Repeat this, holding the pressure of the tongue for a moment so that you feel its contact with the teeth ridge, and notice the explosion on the release of the tongue. No air should escape while you are holding the consonant, only on release, and then it should not be jerky – not too little, not too much – if you put your hand in front of your mouth you will be able to hear it and so judge better.

Now exercise it rhythmically:

tah	tah	tah	tah
tetete	tetete	tetete	tah

c) With the same position and the same pressure as for 't', say 'dah'. Repeat, holding the pressure of the tongue for a moment so that you feel the beginning of the vibrations, still being conscious of those vibrations, and aware of the tongue impelling the sound out:

dah	dah	dah	dah
dedede	dedede	dedede	dah

Keep the movements precise.

d) Again with the tongue in the same position, but this time with the back of the soft palate lowered to allow the sound to come out through the nose, say 'nah'. Repeat, holding the pressure of the tongue for a moment so the sound comes down through the nose, then with clean sound say:

nah	nah	nah	nah
nenene	nenene	nenene	nah

It is important to feel this sound as muscularly firm for this sound as for 'd', and the vowel should be free of nasal resonance — it should be clean. If you find this difficult, alternate it with 'd' like this:

> dedede   nenene   dedede   nenene

or with 't':

> tetete   nenene   tetete   nenene

With all these exercises, do them a few times with the prop first, and then without.

3 *Back of the tongue and soft palate* Exercising these two sets of muscles, as I said at the end of the last chapter, is not only important for clarity, but for the release of the sound through the mouth, and to allow the chest and neck resonators to contribute. If the back of the tongue or soft palate are tight or fixed, it holds the sound in the back, and cuts the tone in half, as it were. You will find that tension in the palate very often goes with tension in the upper lip. Say a few lines of something, consciously keeping the upper lip immobile, and you will find that the back of the palate goes rigid and will notice the effect on the sound. Also, if these two sets of muscles (the palate and the back of tongue) are slack, it gives a thickness to the speech particularly noticeable in Cockney, and even if the vowels are standard, but the muscles slack, it will still give that sound quality which stamps the speech.

Any tension in the back of the soft palate affects the tone considerably, putting a metallic skin on the tone, and making it sound inflexible.

e) To exercise, first of all press the back of the tongue against the soft palate — in fact it is the uvula which is the part that moves — say 'ke' and 'ge'.

Experiment with the pressure of the tongue. If you press the tongue too far up the sound will be tense, if it is too slack the uvula has to drop down too far and the sound will be messy, if you make the contact too far back the sound will be throaty. Try all these positions. Now try to judge the right pressure — the soft palate meeting the back of the tongue, and the contact firm and the release not jerky. Listen with your hand in front:

> kekeke   kekeke   kekeke   kah
> gegege   gegege   gegege   gah

With the 'g' you should feel vibration between the tongue and
   uvula.
   Do this with and without the prop.
f) Repeat the exercise for freeing the tone:

ge	–	with the tongue tensed up and tight
ge	–	with the tongue free but firm
AH	–	with the vowel open and free
ke	–	tight
ke	–	free
AY	–	jaw open and tongue free
ng	–	tight
ng	–	free
I	–	jaw open and tongue free

Those three vowels 'AH', 'AY' and 'I' are good to use because you
   get a feeling of openness from them. Make sure the back of the
   neck is free.

4 *The Lips*   With the prop in to begin with, and then out:
a) Press the whole of the lips together, so that they cover each other
   and you feel their pressure: Say 'pah' and then 'bah', feeling
   the sounds explode outwards.

b) Then not so exaggerated, but still firm:

pepepe	pepepe	pepepe	pah
bebebe	bebebe	bebebe	bah

Feel the lips contributing their own vibration and resonance on 'b'.
c) Do the same with 'm', getting the lip movement as firm as for 'b',
   so that it is muscularly firm, then you will cut down the possibility of the vowel being nasal – it is only when you get general
   mask resonance that the sound is nasal – when it is focussed on
   the lips it will not be.

mememe	mememe	mememe	mah

Then alternate 'm' and 'b':

bebebe	mememe	bebebe	mememe

As I said earlier in the book, the involvement of the lips in speech
is directly related to a sense of sharing what you have to say, so it is

important that they are muscularly alive, for then they will give their own dimension of sound to the speech — this has nothing to do with any exaggerated movement, it is simply that they are toned up and involved. Immobility in the lips actually gives the impression of reluctance to speak.

Also take particular notice of the upper lip to see that it is as involved as the lower one. I have already said that immobility there makes the back of the palate fixed, because the two are muscularly connected, and the involvement of the top lip makes a direct contribution to the tone.

It is interesting to notice that in a strong Australian accent the upper lip is totally immobile, which makes the jaw tight, and all the speech happens in the back of the mouth — the tongue has to work really hard to define the vowels in that limited space. I think this kind of speech, with its almost deliberate uninvolvement or casualness is actually saying, 'I am tough', and it seems to me this is definitely connected with the need to seem tough and virile. Certainly an Australian thinks of an English accent as being cissy or 'poofy', or whatever you like to call it. Some types of American speech have this quality too. It is a kind of signal that you are sending out. I have already talked at length about English upper-class speech, for it too has a lack of mobility in the lips and is defensively unemotional, though the accent itself is different.

We have exercised the different parts of the tongue and the lips, and the consonants which we need for clarity. Now exercise the continuant consonants in pairs, being aware of the difference between breathed and voiced sounds, and getting a lot of sensation and tingling on the voiced ones:

s   —   z (feel the tongue vibrating)
sh —   ge
f   —   v (continue the 'v' to feel the lip vibration)
th —   th   —   voiced   —   (again continue to feel the vibration)

These are excellent to help place the sound in the mouth. You can have a good deal of resonance in the head and face, particularly if you have done a lot of singing, but the resonance is in the face as a whole — or mask — and though all that resonance is valuable and adds to the sound, ultimately it is the verbal energy that impinges, so that finding the vibration on these voiced continuant consonants helps you to focus the energy on the word.

5 *Now for the Vowels*

First exercise the lip vowels, becoming conscious of the muscles that work the lips.

a)   AH   OO

The tongue and palate should be quite free and open – just the lips moving from an open position to a rounded one. Do it several times with the prop in to see how much movement you can get, then with it out. Do not let the lips slur into 'OO', try and get a clean sound without any kind of 'er' in front of it.

b) Then: AH   AW   OO

Feel the tone coming to the muscular action, so that the tone is, as it were, sent out by the lips.

c) Then: AH   AW   OH   OO

Feel the diphthongal movement on 'OH' – make sure the tongue is absolutely free, especially at the back, as that can alter the sound of the vowel.

Feel the precise movement of the lips, so each sound is defined. You should feel a hollow at the back of the tongue. Place the sound specifically on the vowel.

d) Now put vowels and consonants together:

MAH	MAW	MOH	MOO
PAH	PAW	POH	POO
BAH	BAW	BOH	BOO
LAH	LAW	LOH	LOO

Allow the consonant to go firmly but smoothly into the vowel.

e) Do this exercise without the prop – it is really just for loosening up. Do it with an exaggerated movement of the lips and jaw:

                              OI   OW

For 'OI' make the first 'AW' sound very clear before going into 'i'.

Then: MOI   MOW
                       POI   POW
                       BOI   BOW

This is excellent for feeling lip movement.

f) Now we will exercise the tongue vowels. With the prop in say:

                              AH   EE

Repeat this, becoming aware of the tongue moving from a flat position to a highly arched forward position. Take care to keep the tip of the tongue resting on the bottom teeth, or it will interfere with the movement – it is important to feel the blade of the tongue moving separately.

g) With the tip of the tongue still, and first with the prop, then without:

              AH   AY   EE   I

The sounds 'AY' and 'I' are diphthongal, so you should feel the
blade of the tongue move as you say them. It will be easier to
feel on 'I' as it is a bigger movement, starting at 'u' where the
tongue is nearly flat and then arching quite high. A lot of
Cockney 'I' sounds are too far back and start on a back 'AH'
sound — you need to get the front of the tongue working.
'AY' is quite often a tight sound with little movement to it —
if this is so then say the two component sounds separately
several times — 'e' — 'i' — and then try to glide them together.
But it does not matter what variations you have, so long as you
can feel the freedom of the tongue working separately.
Repeat those vowels, conscious that the tongue also provides
resonance, and getting the feeling that the tongue is sending
out the sounds — that it has energy.
h) Put the vowels together with a consonant, feeling the consonant
firm but not jerky:

LAH	LAY	LEE	LI
TAH	TAY	TEE	TI
DAH	DAY	DEE	DI
NAH	NAY	NEE	NI
BAH	BAY	BEE	BI

i) Without the prop, exercise the tongue on the two diphthongs —
exaggerate the movement and get everything very open:

| AY | I |
| LAY | LI |

These two vowels are very liberating for the tone, and I use them a
lot in conjunction with breathing exercises.
j) Still using the blade of the tongue, only this time going in the
reverse direction — from a high arched to a neutral position:

EER	AIR
LEER	LAIR
DEAR	DAIR
TEAR	TAIR
NEAR	NAIR
BEER	BAIR

It is interesting, when trying to write vowel sounds without a
phonetic alphabet, to see just how illogical our spelling system
is.

We have now gone through all the movements of the vowels and
consonants — they will vary with your accent, but that does not

matter, what matters is that you become aware of the possibilities of movement, and that you find the energy in these muscles.

As with the breathing exercises, you will know what you need particularly — in most cases it is a matter of stimulating the muscles so that they work for you, and do not act as a kind of wall between your thoughts and your words, or you and us.

Now let us try some of this out on a piece of text. I know a lot of people use patter exercises, like Gilbert and Sullivan verses, or a tongue-twister. I personally do not think they have much value — you learn to do them, but because they mean nothing to your intelligence or feeling, they do not relate to your ordinary speech. And in any case they have no weight. Try this extract from Dylan Thomas's *Under Milk Wood.* The whole play is tremendous to read aloud, though of course a lot of it is very Welsh, but I think the First and Second Voices can be read without a Welsh accent, and, because the language is so physical and muscularly alive, it illustrates, without explaining, the whole business of words being movement. Just the act of speaking it teaches us something.

I enclose here an extract, spoken by the First and Second Voices. Avoid any Welsh accent as it will take away from the point of the exercise, which is for you to feel your mouth — your tongue, your lips and palate — in action.

First, make sure you have a good free posture, and open out your breathing for a moment — then do not worry about it. Do it first — slowly — with the prop in, noticing all the movements that you are making. This passage gives a description of Lord Cut-Glass, who is a rather eccentric inhabitant of this mad Welsh town.

From *UNDER MILK WOOD*

First voice: Lord Cut-Glass, in his kitchen full of time, squats down alone to a dogdish, marked Fido, of peppery fish-scraps and listens to the voices of his sixty-six clocks, one for each year of his loony age, and watches, with love, their black-and-white moony loud-lipped faces tocking the earth away: slow clocks, quick clocks, pendulumed heart-knocks, china, alarm, grandfather, cuckoo; clocks shaped like Noah's whirring Ark, clocks that bicker in marble ships, clocks in the wombs of glass women, hourglass chimers, tu-wit-tu-woo clocks, clocks that pluck tunes, Vesuvius clocks all black bells and lava, Niagara clocks that cataract their ticks, old time-weeping clocks with ebony beards, clocks with no hands for ever drumming out time without ever knowing what time it is. His sixty-six singers are all set at different hours. Lord Cut-Glass lives in a house and a life at siege. Any minute or dark day now, the unknown enemy will loot and savage downhill, but they will not catch him napping. Sixty-six different times in his fish-slimy kitchen ping, strike, tick, chime, and tock.

Second voice: The lust and lilt and lather and emerald breeze and crackle of the bird-praise and body of Spring with its breasts full of rivering May-milk, means, to that lordly fish-head nibbler, nothing but another nearness to the tribes and navies of the Last Black Day who'll sear and pillage down Armageddon Hill to his double-locked rusty-shuttered tick-tock dust-scrabbled shack at the bottom of the town that has fallen head over bells in love.

Dylan Thomas

What marvellous descriptions they are, packed with imagery and full of warmth and irony and wit, yet with a certain savagery underlying it. For you are aware of the passion of Dylan Thomas's feeling through the particular words he uses. It is like that with all his writing – it makes you aware of the tie-up between the emotional depth and the physical make-up of words.

You might find it difficult to do the whole of one passage with a prop in, so take it out when it gets too much – do a little at a time, first with it in, and then with it out. What matters is not pace but precision – completing all the words and feeling the movement of each vowel and consonant. So to begin with do it very slowly.

The first passage is tricky to say, make sure you get all the ends of the words clear – e.g., 'loudlipped faces' – 'clocks shaped like Noah's whirring Ark' etc., do not skip or slide over one sound. It will then make you aware of how much one does slide over in everyday speech. The second passage has heavier sounds – more voiced consonants and longer vowels – e.g., 'slumbers and voyages' – make sure the voiced consonants are fully voiced, particularly the final 's' sounds which are always pronounced 'z' after another voiced consonant or after a vowel. Words like 'brawls' – 'dark dock bars'– 'twines and souses with the drowned and blowzy-breasted dead' – all those vowel sounds are really long and have movement in them – 'AW', 'AH', 'OW', 'I'.

First, then, experiment with it slowly, with and without the prop. Then take the prop out and speak one of the passages, again fairly slowly, exaggerating the movement of the jaw, so that it opens more than normally, and all the sounds will, consequently, be exaggerated.

Sometimes, cup your hands round your mouth, under the nose, so that they act like a megaphone – this helps you to pinpoint the energy in the mouth – when you take your hands away you will find that you can hear the sound springing out. This is valuable to do on any piece of text.

Always end your practice by speaking it quite normally, without exaggeration, but being aware of the influence of the exercises you have done. Gradually begin to focus on the meaning more than on the means. It should start to feel good – so enjoy it.

When you feel you have accomplished something with it, try joining it up with the breathing exercises you have done – but go at it gently, and above all, do not get cross with yourself!

When everything is beginning to work for you, what you should feel is this: the voice starting from the centre on your breath, having a totally free passage through the body and being resonated, and being sent out in the form of words by your tongue, lips and palate. So that it comes straight from the breath to the word – it is those two places that give the energy, and there should be no sense of effort anywhere else.

What you have done is investigate the wholeness of words, the movement in them, and you will have found out the sounds you tend to miss, or slide over, or if you substitute one sound for another because it is easier – the temptation for instance to say 'Lorg-Cut Glass' substituting the consonant 'g' for 'd' because it is made in the same place as 'c'. We do this a lot in colloquial speech. You are not changing your accent, you are simply investigating the muscular activity in words, and making that action more complete. Now it would obviously be incongruous to be as precise as that in your everyday speech, but you will find a balance, and you will be aware of what you are after.

I would just like to say a word about the length of vowels in English, which is extremely interesting, and also makes a difference to speech. We have already seen that some vowels have a longer quality than others, but also that length varies according to the consonant that follows. Breathed plosive consonants – p, t, k – shorten a vowel very much, while voiced consonants take longer to say themselves, and also lengthen the preceding vowel. Voiced continuant consonants take even longer, and more than one lengthens the vowel even more. By speaking them aloud, notice the differing lengths in these sets of words:

sat	–	sad
rate	–	raid
feet	–	feed

leak	–	leaf
lead	–	leave
fit	–	fill
caught	–	call
lad	–	lamb

A continuant consonant lengthens more than a plosive, and a voiced consonant lengthens more than a breathed one. But combinations of consonants make even more difference:

heart	– hard	– harm	– harms		
hat	– had	– hand	– hands		
leak	– leaf	– lead	– leads	– leave	– leaves
set	– said	– sell	– self	– selves	
rate	– raid	– rain	– range	– ranged	

These differences alter the way you say the vowel, and how open it can be – a very short vowel can never be as open as a long one, or as complete in movement.

Now for any specific difficulties you may have.

a) If you find you get a lot of glottal attack on vowels and you find it difficult to place them forward, try this progression of vowel sounds with an 'H' in front. Do it quite slowly so that you feel the tone coming to where you are making the sound – i.e., the lips for the lip vowels, and the blade of the tongue for the tongue vowels:

HOO   HOH   HAW   HAH   HAY   HEE   HOW   HI

Then think the 'H' but do not say it, feeling the breath and the vowel firm and smooth

OO   OH   AW   AH   AY   EE   OW   I

In certain accents glottal stops come in the middle of words – i.e., at the end of the vowel and before the final consonant, so that a word like 'wait', for instance, would have a kind of glottal stop between the 'AY' and the 't' – it is as though the resonance is taken right back into the throat at the end of the vowel sound. This happens notably in certain kinds of Yorkshire accents – particularly when the vowel precedes a 't', a 'p', or a 'k' – unvoiced plosive consonants as in the words 'fat', 'cup', 'back'. It also happens, though with a different effect, in West Indian accents – the vowel gets taken back into the throat, and sometimes even, a glottal stop replaces the consonant. This can also happen with Cockney – 'a cup of tea' – it is possible to say this with a glottal stop replacing the 'p' of 'cup' and the whole of 'of', so you get 'a cu' 'ertea'.

If this is your problem, take the same sequence of vowels with 'M' or 'N' or 'L' behind them, first singing them and then speaking them very smoothly, so that you become conscious of the smooth passage of sound and you realize where you would normally break it and make it jerky. This requires patience, as it is a difficult little habit to break — it is always more difficult to stop doing something, than to get into the habit of doing something. So practise:

OOM OHM AWM AHM AYM EEM OWM IME
OON OHN AWN AHN AYN EEN OWN INE
OOL OHL AWL AHL AYL EEL OWL ILE

When you feel this is smooth, put the vowels to plosive consonants like 't', 'k' and 'p', still keeping the smoothness between the vowel and the consonant.

b) Beginning consonants, you may find they are either too breathy initially, or jerky and hard, making the subsequent vowel sound hard. Try the same sequence of vowels with different consonants in front, experimenting with the right pressure — keep the jaw nice and free, though do it with the prop sometimes:

TOO TOH TAW TAH TAY TEE TOW TI
DOO DOH DAW DAH DAY DEE DOW DI
POO POH PAW PAH PAY PEE POW PI
BOO BOH BAW BAH BAY BEE BOW BI
KOO KOH KAW KAH KAY KEE KOW KI
GOO GOH GAW GAH GAY GEE GOW GI

In each case, feel the consonant springing the vowel out, and the difference between the breathed and voiced consonants.

c) To help the placing of the tone forward in the mouth, and to be aware of the friction of the sound carrying through, do the same with the following continuant consonants — feeling a great deal of vibration with the voiced ones:

FOO   FOH   FAW   FAH   FAY   FEE   FOW   FI
VOO   VOH   VAW   VAH   VAY   VEE   VOW   VI
SOO   SOH   SAW   SAH   SAY   SEE   SOW   SI
ZOO   ZOH   ZAW   ZAH   ZAY   ZEE   ZOW   ZI
THOO THOH THAW THAH THAY THEE THOW THI
(unvoiced as in 'thin')
THOO THOH THAW THAH THAY THEE THOW THI
(voiced as in 'this')

d) End consonants — so often they get left off — they do not in fact need the same impulse of breath as the initial consonants, but they do need to be there:

OOT	OHT	AWT	AHT	AYT	EET	OWT	ITE
OOD	OHD	AWD	AHD	AYD	EED	OWD	IDE
OOP	OHP	AWP	AHP	AYP	EEP	OWP	IPE
OOB	OHB	AWB	AHB	AYB	EEB	OWB	IBE
OOK	OHK	AWK	AHK	AYK	EEK	OWK	IKE
OOG	OHG	AWG	AHG	AYG	EEG	OWG	IGE
OOF	OHF	AWF	AHF	AYF	EEF	OWF	IFE
OOV	OHV	AWV	AHV	AYV	EEV	OWV	IVE
OOS	OHS	AWS	AHS	AYS	EES	OWS	ISE
OOZ	OHZ	AWZ	AHZ	AYZ	EEZ	OWZ	IZE
OOTH	OHTH	AWTH	AHTH	AYTH	EETH	OWTH	ITHE

(breathed)

OOTH	OHTH	AWTH	AHTH	AYTH	EETH	OWTH	ITHE

(voiced)

e) Final 'l' sounds. These are often slid over and not given their full value. It is possible to substitute 'w' for 'l' and get away with it, it is a common substitution in fact. Try it for yourself on the word 'field' — do not say 'l' but substitute 'w' for it, and you will find the word quite recognizable. This is because the dark 'l' has an 'OO' vowel quality.

There are really two kinds of 'l' sounds — a) what we call a light 'l', these we use at the beginning of words or syllables when they come before a vowel. And b) the dark 'l' sounds which come at the end of a word or before another consonant.

For both 'l' sounds, the tip of the tongue is pressed against the teeth ridge, but for the light 'l' the back of the tongue is raised and for the dark 'l' the back of the tongue is lowered. Try these two words out slowly and feel the different position of the back of the tongue: 'leaf' — 'feel'.

In both these words the back of the tongue is raised high for the vowel anyway — the whole tongue is arched up for 'EE' — so that there is quite a time gap in 'feel' for the blade of the tongue to move down from 'EE' to 'l' — this being a dark 'l'. Say 'feel' again and notice the movement and the time it takes — there is almost a small neutral vowel between the two sounds — 'F–EE–er–L'.

You will see that both light and dark 'l's vary their sound according to the vowel that precedes or follows — before a high tongue vowel the light 'l' is lighter, and after a low tongue vowel or a lip vowel, the dark 'l' is extra dark. And when it is what we call a syllabic 'l', as in 'able', where the tongue takes the weight of the vowel, it is at its darkest – i.e., the back of the tongue is lowest.

This sounds complicated, but if you try this sequence of words, you will see exactly what I mean. They go from very light to very dark 'l's:

leaf – loom – eel – cool – able

If you feel your 'l' sounds are not clear, try the following sets of words, making sure that the tip of the tongue is pressed hard against the teeth ridge for both kinds of 'l' – for it is when the tongue tip does not remain firm for dark 'l's that their clarity goes.

feel	–	field	gnarl	–	gnarled
fill	–	filled	fall	–	falls
fail	–	failed – fails	foal	–	fold
sell	–	sells	cool	–	cooled
girl	–	girls	silver	–	milk

You will see that it takes a certain time to say 'l' completely, and it is important that it gets its full value.

f) Difficult combinations of consonants – some people find difficulty in saying two or three consonants together. The best thing is to do them with the sequence of vowels I have just given – sometimes with the prop and sometimes without, though certain consonants cannot be done with it in – 'f', 'v', 'th' – 's' and 'z' cannot be said quite accurately with it, but if it benefits the consonants they are with, then use it. Here are some examples, but you can make up your own drill to suit yourself:

OOKT	OHKT	AWKT	AHKT	AYKT	EEKT	OWKT	IKT
OOGD	OHGD	AWGD	AHGD	AYGD	EEGD	OWGD	IGD
OOPT	OHPT	AWPT	AHPT	AYPT	EEPT	OWPT	IPT
OOBD	OHBD	AWBD	AHBD	AYBD	EEBD	OWBD	IBD
OOTHT	OHTHT	AWTHT	AHTHT	AYTHT	EETHT	OWTHT	ITHT
OOTHD	OHTHD	AWTHD	AHTHD	AYTHD	EETHD	OWTHD	ITHD
OOST	OHST	AWST	AHST	AYST	EEST	OWST	IST
OOZD	OHZD	AWZD	AHZD	AYZD	EEZD	OWZD	IZD
OOKST	OHKST	AWKST	AHKST	AYKST	EEKST	OWKST	IKST

(This happens in words like 'mixed', 'waxed' etc.)

OOSKT	OHSKT	AWSKT	AHSKT	AYSKT	EESKT	OWSKT	ISKT

(For 'asked', 'whisked' etc.)

OOFT	OHFT	AWFT	AHFT	AYFT	EEFT	OWFT	IFT
OOVD	OHVD	AWVD	AHVD	AYVD	EEVD	OWVD	IVD

This is a fairly good selection, but you can add to it.

One thing to remember, if you feel that you need to make your speech clearer, is that the tendency is often to overdo it, and become too precise so that it sounds formal. For instance, when you have two words, the first ending with the same sound as the next begins with as in 'want to or could do', you do not say the 't' or 'd' twice, you hang onto them a split second longer than if it were one sound, that is all. It must always sound quite natural.

g) Over nasality. As I have said, this comes when the nasal resonance from the nasal consonants, 'm', 'n' and 'ng', spills over into the vowels and colours the tone. But you can also have some tone which is nasal of itself, and this is because the palate at the back is slack and not cutting off the nasal passage firmly enough. There should always be a certain amount of nasal resonance, otherwise the tone becomes dry and would sound as if you had a perpetual cold, but it should be limited, and if the back of the palate is muscularly firm, it will be. To get it free of nasality you can try this:

kekeke – then 'AH' very open (almost like a yawn to feel the palate high at the back)

gegege – then 'AY' in the same way

Breathe in sharply and quickly through the mouth, noticing the cold air hitting the back of the palate, and then say an open vowel like 'AH' or 'AY' immediately, noticing the feeling of the high palate – this cuts out too much nasal resonance, and will make the palate firmer.

Then, with the sequence of vowels already given, put 'm' and 'n' before and after them:

MOO   MOH, etc.
NOO   NOH, etc.
OOM   OHM, etc.
OON   OHN, etc.
OOMZ OHMZ, etc.

Then say words with nasal consonants like 'moon', 'moan', 'mood' etc., getting the feeling that the vowel is open and springing through the mouth. If you find this difficult, alternate it with 'd' and 'b', thus:

boon – moon – noon
dome – mode – moan

or any similar combination.

Just as with breathing, there is great value in doing exercises for muscularity and moving around at the same time. I hope the exercises already given will make you want to say words aloud, because that is perhaps the main part of the whole process. Just as a suggestion, here is a poem by Edith Sitwell from her *Façade* suite, which has been set to music by William Walton — or rather he composed music for the poems to be spoken to. All the poems in this suite are very rhythmical, but their usefulness is not only in that, for they are full of imagery, admittedly a rather private imagery of the poet's own, but the sound and weight of the words play an important part in the pictures painted — as a poet she was very concerned with the thicknesses and thinnesses of words — their whole texture. Try this one, which is written to the rhythm of a foxtrot. Learn part of it, so that you can dance round to its rhythm while saying the words. Keep the diction precise. As you move to its rhythm and feel it in your body, you will find lots of things happening in the voice as you speak — changes of rhythm in the words and more flexibility in the inflection. Go on dancing to it until you feel this buoyancy and freedom coming into your voice.

FOX TROT

Old
> Sir
>> Faulk,
> Tall as a stork,
Before the honeyed fruits of dawn were ripe, would walk,
And stalk with a gun
The reynard-coloured sun,
Among the pheasant-feathered corn the unicorn has torn, forlorn the
Smock-faced sheep
Sit
> And
>> Sleep;
Periwigged as William and Mary, weep . . .
'Sally, Mary, Mattie, what's the matter, why cry?'
The huntsman and the reynard-coloured sun and I sigh;

'Oh, the nursery-maid Meg
With a leg like a peg
Chased the feathered dreams like hens, and when they laid an egg
In the sheepskin
Meadows
Where
The serene King James would steer
Horse and hounds, then he
From the shade of a tree
Picked it up as spoil to boil for nursery tea,' said the mourners. In the
Corn, towers strain,
Feathered tall as a crane,
And whistling down the feathered rain, old Noah goes again —
An old dull mome
With a head like a pome,
Seeing the world as a bare egg,
Laid by the feathered air; Meg
Would beg three of these
For the nursery teas
Of Japhet, Shem, and Ham; she gave it
Underneath the trees,
Where the boiling
    Water
        Hissed,
Like the goose-king's feathered daughter — kissed
Pot and pan and copper kettle
Put upon their proper mettle,
Lest the Flood — the Flood — the Flood begin again through these!

Edith Sitwell

The more you do this, the more it will grow on you — there is a
mad logic in it. Only do a part of it at a time, feel each syllable
become very precise, and let the rhythm of the words act on you as
a piece of '30s dance music might, so that you want to dance to it. It
is nice to do.

I would like to end this chapter with two pieces of writing in which
the sound of the words is part of their meaning in a deep sense. When
you speak them you know their need for verbal energy. Both are
metaphysical poems — always in metaphysical writing one is aware of
man's cosmic position — i.e., man's relation to the universe.

The Marvell poem begins with a lighthearted plea to his mistress to go to bed with him, and you can hear the verbal wit in the words and his play with their sounds — 'And you should if you please refuse/ Till the Conversion of the Jews.', etc., or 'My vegetable Love . . .'. But in the middle section it gets serious, the sound changes, and part through sound and part through sense, we are made aware of our mortality — 'then Worms shall try/ That long preserv'd Virginity:' The words take on a different sound. The last section is different again and more urgent in sound. All the argument is conveyed through an extraordinary balance of sound and sense — requiring verbal awareness.

The second piece is a sonnet by John Donne, asking God to take over his soul. The argument is written in physically powerful terms — 'Batter my heart . . ' 'bend . . . and make me new.' 'I, like an usurpt towne . . ./Labour to' admit you,.' . . . for I/Except you'enthrall mee, never shall be free,/Nor ever chaste, except you ravish mee.' The images are really quite startling, and to end with the word 'ravish', with its sexual implications, is extraordinary. The point is, it again makes you aware of the physical nature of the word, for to find the depth and strength of his religious feeling, you have to deal with those words in their three-dimensional sense. We understand something of the power of his feelings by the words he chooses.

TO HIS COY MISTRESS

Had we but world enough, and Time,
This coyness Lady were no crime.
We would sit down, and think which way
To walk, and pass our long Loves Day.
Thou by the *Indian Ganges* side
Should'st Rubies find: I by the tide
Of *Humber* would complain. I would
Love you ten years before the Flood:
And you should if you please refuse
Till the Conversion of the *Jews*.

My vegetable Love should grow
Vaster than Empires, and more slow.
An hundred years should go to praise
Thine Eyes, and on thy Forehead Gaze,
Two hundred to adore each Breast:
But thirty thousand to the rest;
An Age at least to every part,
And the last Age should show your Heart.
For, Lady, you deserve this State,
Nor would I love at lower rate.
   But at my back I alwaies hear
Times winged Charriot hurrying near:
And yonder all before us lye
Desarts of vast Eternity.
Thy Beauty shall no more be found;
Nor, in thy marble Vault shall sound
My ecchoing song: then Worms shall try
That long preserv'd Virginity:
And your quaint Honour turn to dust;
And into ashes all my Lust.
The Grave's a fine and private place,
But none, I think, do there embrace.
   Now therefore, while the youthful hew
Sits on thy skin like morning dew,
And while thy willing Soul transpires
At every pore with instant Fires,
Now let us sport us while we may;
And now, like am'rous birds of prey,
Rather at once our Time devour
Than languish in his slow-chapt pow'r.
Let us roll all our Strength and all
Our sweetness up into one Ball,
And tear our Pleasures with rough strife,
Thorough the Iron gates of Life.
Thus, though we cannot make our Sun
Stand still, yet we will make him run.

Andrew Marvell

SONNET XIV

Batter my heart, three person'd God; for, you
As yet but knocke, breathe, shine, and seeke to mend;
That I may rise, and stand, o'erthrow mee,' and bend
Your force, to breake, blowe, burn and make me new.
I, like an usurpt towne, to'another due,
Labour to'admit you, but Oh, to no end,
Reason your viceroy in mee, mee should defend,
But is captiv'd, and proves weake or untrue.
Yet dearely'I love you, and would be loved faine,
But am betroth'd unto your enemie:
Divorce mee, untie, or break that knot againe,
Take mee to you, imprison mee, for I
Except you'enthrall mee, never shall be free,
Nor ever chaste, except you ravish mee.

John Donne

8
Tone, Projection and Variety

You have now exercised the voice fairly fully and will have found what exercises work best for you, and, hopefully, you will have been surprised — pleasantly of course — by some of the sound you have found. Do persevere with the exercises, though, for the more they get into the system the more readily the voice will respond and reflect your intentions. Not the least valuable thing will be that you will have thought objectively about your voice, and you will have an understanding of how it works, and this quite simple orientation of thought can give you enormous confidence.

What I am sure of, is that the exercises cannot fail, for they are all really the result of common sense, and all you are doing is extending physical resources that already exist. The difference will be noticeable immediately, so that you will hear it in your everyday speech.

Through the breathing exercises you find more vocal energy, and through the speech exercises you focus that energy onto the word — for it is the word that gathers all you are thinking and feeling, and communicates it to others. If you are over-emphatic in your speech — on the offensive as it were — it puts people off, if you are not positive enough, you do not reach. It is a matter of getting the balance right.

Consequently, the more you try to put the two sets of energy together, the more satisfactory the voice will be. In other words, read out loud a lot.

Just one small word of caution, just as I said it was important to check with a doctor on vocal fatigue, so, if you are bothered by any sort of defect, such as difficulty in making 'r' and 's' sounds, or anything like a stammer or stutter, this must be dealt with by a speech therapist. I have not attempted to give directions for 'r's or 's's, because you cannot do this second-hand, it should be done through a qualified therapist. If it is a slight defect, then I would not worry about it, but if it bothers you, find someone who can help.

Another thing is that new false teeth often cause a deal of bother. There is nothing you can do, except patiently exercise the tongue and lips — for they often make you fix the lips out of tension — but I would not attempt to use a bone-prop.

Placing and Tone When you feel the exercises are working well for you, and you are not having to think so hard about what every part of you is doing, take time to think of your body as a whole, resonating the sound.

a) Take, say, the first verse of 'The glories of our blood and state' or the Shakespeare sonnet, sit on the floor and rock quite hard, forwards and backwards on your seat. Concentrate the sound on the base of your spine so that you feel the vibrations there. Do this for several minutes.

b) Standing up, jog about weightily and say the same verse, this time concentrating on your back, aware of the resonance there. Also, lean heavily against a wall and concentrate the resonance in the back, feeling its vibrations on the wall.

c) Then put one hand on your chest, and add that vibration – so that you feel the resonance beginning to accumulate.

d) Consciously relax your jaw, and with it the back of your tongue, and feel all the space in your neck and behind the tongue adding to the sound. I do stress that it is crucial to have as free a jaw as possible.

e) Now, with your hands, massage your cheeks quite vigorously, so that you feel all of that part of your face alive. Then speak the verse and feel the resonance.

f) Then put one hand on the top of your head, and hum, then speak, and feel the vibrations in the skull.

g) Now, cup your hands round your mouth and say 'VVV' until you feel all the vibrations on the lips, and 'ZZZ' until you feel your whole head vibrating, and then the soft 'GE' (as in measure) this actually makes your ears tingle – and then speak the verse.

Now speak anything you like, aware of the breathing working for you, aware of the potential resonance, and letting the voice go anywhere it likes. So, you start to feel freedom of pitch.

Projection With that resonance in mind, think about focussing on different objects at different distances – we did this before with humming and singing vowels.

a) Experiment by throwing vowel sounds at three different objects, one close, one medium distance and one quite far. First breathe in and then, on the outgoing breath, get a sense of throwing the vowel out – pitching it – you can back this up by throwing an imaginary ball with your arm. Pitch the vowel out – use long open vowels like 'AH' and 'AY'.

b) Take a piece of text, preferably a piece of narrative so that there is quite a lot of pitch variety in it, and do the same with that – focus a few lines near, and then further away, and so on. Try

110

not to do this so much by increasing the volume, but by mentally reaching out to that object — the voice actually carries there if your intention is strong enough behind it — but certainly be sure you do not pitch it higher as you increase the distance. When you are speaking to people it should be easier, providing you never lose the sense of talking to someone — I know that sounds a simple thing to say, but it is these simple things that so often escape you when faced with a daunting situation.

One very important thing you will notice is that projection has a great deal to do with the time you allow for your sound to reach — some part of you has got to be constantly aware of the time it takes for thought and words to reach a distance, and that time has to do with allowing the vowels to carry, and giving time to the consonants to make an impact. If I simply said go slower, that would not be the answer, for then it would drag, and your thinking has always got to be ahead and leading — allow time for your thought to follow through. I remember, when learning tennis, I was taught to follow the ball through — it did not do much good as I seldom hit the ball in the first place, but in fact that is what you have got to do with your words. Pitch them out, and allow them to reach.

Variety

Because of all the things we have discussed — habit, use, ear etc. — some people have a natural variety in their voice and some do not. If you have you instinctively use it, but if you have not then you have to develop it. Some people enjoy talking more than others, and also have a sense of performance — this has nothing to do with acting, some people do enjoy telling stories and anecdotes and being witty. And, of course, the best public speakers very often have a theatrical sense — they know how to build suspense, they know when to pause and when to make sudden changes in volume and pitch — we all recognise this quality and are entertained by it, whether we are agreeing with the content or not.

To speak well you do not want to put anything on or try for this kind of theatrical presentation, for that would be false. At the same time you recognize that change or surprise is needed vocally if people are to be interested, so we have to find ways of gradually extending your range and it is a gradual process, for, to begin with, using more range will sound false to you and, as with fuller tone, you have to get used to it and make it a part of you. But variety must never be used for its own sake, it must come out of the need to express more accurately and communicate more completely. So how do we go about it?

First of all, to be practical, I suppose there are four technical
means at your disposal. I do not like to talk about it technically,
because it implies contrivance, but it might just make you aware of
the possibilities. They are:

  i)   Changes of pitch and inflection
  ii) Changes of pace
  iii) Use of pause
  iv) Changes in volume

It is interesting to notice that in ordinary conversation with
people whom you know well, you will find the voice has all these
qualities, though maybe on a miniature scale. But, directly you are
in a more formal situation, or are faced with having to speak louder,
these natural shades of variation disappear, or become swamped by
the extra volume. To bridge that gap, we have, as with the other voice
areas, to find material which cries out for variety of all sorts, and
then read it aloud and just experiment. Then you will find a) what
you have got, and b) that it is possible to use that variety without
being false — that you are only extending yourself.

The best material to use for this is narrative. There is great value
in getting the sense of unfolding a story — keeping a suspense going —
also by reading good prose you hear how other people use rhythms,
and how they communicate what they feel and what they do, so
that it opens up your own ways and means, and makes you aware
of the possibilities in your own voice. Incidentally, reading stories
to children is marvellous, because you feel free to be a bit outrageous,
and the more outrageous you are, the more they love it — it can
make you aware of a lot of range.

To illustrate what I mean about narrative, I am including, here,
one passage from Dickens, an extract from a poem by George
Crabbe, a poem by Dylan Thomas and a passage from Joyce's *A
Portrait of the Artist as a Young Man.* I will make a few points about
each one of them.

Read any passage from Dickens aloud, and you cannot fail to
learn something from it. Rythmically it is so alive and full of change,
because of the enormous variety of length in the phrases he uses,
and their elasticity. His imagination alights maybe on one object or
element and elaborates on it with such remarkable invention, that
it surprises you every time you read it. He builds his descriptions
with such detail that the cumulative result is almost overwhelming.
This passage from *Bleak House* is written in note form — a kind
of shorthand — which gives it particular immediacy, and his
description of fog contains some most outlandish humour — people

on a bridge looking down into a 'nether sky' as if they were in a balloon. But you will see all this. The point is, the fog goes everywhere — and so can your voice, if you listen for what those lines do. Try not to decide beforehand how to read it, but read it allowing yourself to be surprised, so that your voice is taken off-guard, as it were, and reacts in a way that you do not plan. That is the value.

The extract from the long poem called *The Parish Register* is also good, but in another, more precise and exacting, way. It was written by George Crabbe, who was a Church of England clergyman in the late eighteenth and early nineteenth centuries, and eventually became rector of Trowbridge in Wiltshire. The poem is in three parts — Baptisms, Marriages, and Burials — this passage obviously coming from the first part. The characters in the poem were real, though he disguised their identity. This is a particularly nice passage, I think, for there is no sentimentality, it has a splendid pithy humour, coupled with real compassion and commonsense advice. It is quite difficult, written as it is in strict metre and rhyming couplets, so that you have to find rhythmic variety within that strict form, and to do that you find you have to use more inflection. Though metrically it is so strict, you will find that there are many permutations of rhythm in the lines — that is to say some of the lines run on, as does the very first line, so that you hold up 'grace', in order to give more weight to the subject — i.e., 'the Miller's Daughter'. But the line — 'And not presume — without his leave — to love' has a quite different rhythm and cadence to make its point. So play about with the lines, investigate the words and allow them to act on you. You also have to observe the discipline of the narrative, so that vocally you have to be continually leading us on. And you must also have the particular attitude to the story which Crabbe held, for it is the way he tells the story that makes it interesting, the pithy comments he makes, and the dry, unsentimental, but feeling caution he gives us at the end. There is a lot for the voice to do.

The Hunchback in the Park is marvellous, just for sound — I have put it in because I like it so much. It also is a good vocal discipline in that you have to keep its plot going — i.e., what happens to the hunchback — and make it clear, although it is told to us in compressed, shorthand images. Also there is very little punctuation, so that you have to keep the sense going through the inflections, for two verses, managing all the parentheses, until the first full stop. Really the sense goes — 'The hunchback in the park/. . . Slept at night in a dog kennel/But nobody chained him up.' And all the part in between — 'A solitary mister/Propped,' etc. — are the impressions that Dylan Thomas wants us to get. Again, in the last section, the sense goes from — 'And the old dog sleeper/ . . . Made all day until bell time/A woman figure without fault'. I like the way the images of boys and dogs and swans and strawberries interweave, and the extraordinary poignancy of a hunchback carving a perfect female figure.

The last passage, the extract from Joyce's semi-autobiographical novel, is part of a sermon preached by one of the Jesuits at Stephen's school. Stephen Dedalus – or Joyce – is recalling one of the sermons that were preached to frighten the students away from the sins of the flesh. It is a splendid piece of rhetorical writing, in that it builds, through repetition and detail, to a climax, then it drops right away again only to lead you to greater climax and emotional involvement. Of course, there is humour in that we are hearing it via the experience of the central character.

From *BLEAK HOUSE*

Chapter I   In Chancery

London. Michaelmas Term lately over, and the Lord Chancellor sitting in Lincoln's Inn Hall. Implacable November weather. As much mud in the streets, as if the waters had but newly retired from the face of the earth, and it would not be wonderful to meet a Megalosaurus, forty feet long or so, waddling like an elephantine lizard up Holborn Hill. Smoke lowering down from chimney-pots, making a soft black drizzle, with flakes of soot in it as big as full-grown snow-flakes – gone into mourning, one might imagine, for the death of the sun. Dogs, undistinguishable in mire. Horses, scarcely better; splashed to their very blinkers. Foot-passengers jostling one another's umbrellas, in a general infection of ill-temper, and losing their foothold at street-corners, where tens of thousands of other foot-passengers have been slipping and sliding since the day broke (if this day ever broke), adding new deposits to the crust upon crust of mud, sticking at those points tenaciously to the pavement, and accumulating at compound interest.

Fog everywhere. Fog up the river, where it flows among green aits and meadows; fog down the river, where it rolls defiled among the tiers of shipping, and the waterside pollutions of a great (and dirty) city. Fog on the Essex marshes, fog on the Kentish heights. Fog creeping into the cabooses of collier-brigs, fog lying out on the yards, and hovering in the rigging of great ships; fog drooping on the gunwales of barges and small boats. Fog in the eyes and throats of ancient Greenwich pensioners, wheezing by the firesides of their wards; fog in the stem and bowl of the afternoon pipe of the wrathful skipper, down in his close cabin; fog cruelly pinching the toes and fingers of his shivering little 'prentice boy on deck. Chance people on the bridges peeping over the parapets into a nether sky of fog, with fog all round them, as if they were up in a balloon, and hanging in the misty clouds.

Gas looming through the fog in divers places in the streets, much as the sun may, from the spongy fields, be seen to loom by husbandman and ploughboy. Most of the shops lighted two hours before their time — as the gas seems to know, for it has a haggard and unwilling look.

The raw afternoon is rawest, and the dense fog is densest, and the muddy streets are muddiest, near that leaden-headed old obstruction, appropriate ornament for the threshold of a leaden-headed old corporation: Temple Bar. And hard by Temple Bar, in Lincoln's Inn Hall, at the very heart of the fog, sits the Lord High Chancellor in his High Court of Chancery.

Charles Dickens

From *THE PARISH REGISTER*

Of all the Nymphs who gave our Village grace,
The Miller's daughter had the fairest face:
Proud was the Miller; money was his pride,
He rode to market, as our farmers ride,
And 'twas his boast, inspired by spirits, there,
His favourite Lucy should be rich as fair;
But she must meek and still obedient prove,
And not presume, without his leave, to love.
    A youthful Sailor heard him; — "Ha!" quoth he,
This Miller's maiden is the prize for me;
Her charms I love, his riches I desire,
And all his threats but fan the kindling fire;
My ebbing purse, no more the foe shall fill,
But Love's kind act and Lucy at the Mill."
    Thus thought the youth, and soon the chase began,
Stretch'd all his sail, nor thought of pause or plan;
His trusty staff in his bold hand he took,
Like him and like his frigate, heart of oak;
Fresh were his features, his attire was new;
Clean was his linen and his jacket blue;
Of finest jean, his trowsers, tight and trim,
Brush'd the large buckle at the silver rim.
    He soon arrived, he traced the village-green,
There saw the maid, and was with pleasure seen;
Then talked of love, till Lucy's yielding heart
Confess'd 'twas painful, though 'twas right to part.
    "For ah! my Father has a haughty soul,
Whom best he loves, he loves but to control;
Me to some churl in bargain he'll consign,
And make some tyrant of the parish mine;
Cold is his heart, and he with looks severe
Has often forced, but never shed the tear;
Save, when my mother died, some drops express'd
A kind of sorrow for a wife at rest:—
To me a master's stern regard is shown,
I'm like his steed, prized highly as his own;
Stroked but corrected, threatened when supplied,
His slave and boast, his victim and his pride."
    "Cheer up, my lass! I'll to thy father go,
The Miller cannot be the Sailor's foe;
Both live by Heaven's free gale that plays aloud
In the stretched canvas and the piping shroud;

The rush of winds, the flapping sails above,
And rattling planks within, are sounds *we* love;
Calms are our dread; when tempests plough the deep
We take a reef, and to the rocking sleep."

"Ha!" quoth the Miller, moved at speech so rash,
Art thou like me? then where thy notes and cash?
Away to Wapping, and a wife command,
With all thy wealth, a guinea, in thine hand;
There with thy messmates quaff the muddy cheer,
And leave my Lucy for thy betters here."

"Revenge! revenge!" the angry lover cried,
Then sought the nymph, and "Be thou now my bride."
Bride had she been, but they no priest could move
To bind in law, the couple bound by love.

What sought these lovers then by day, by night?
But stolen moments of disturb'd delight;
Soft trembling tumults, terrors dearly prized,
Transports that pained and joys that agonised:
Till, the fond damsel, pleased with lad so trim,
Awed by her parent and enticed by him,
Her lovely form from savage power to save,
Gave — not her hand — but ALL she could, she gave.

Then came the day of shame, the grievous night,
The varying look, the wondering appetite;
The joy assumed, while sorrow dimm'd the eyes,
The forced sad smiles that follow'd sudden sighs;
And every art, long used, but used in vain,
To hide thy progress, Nature, and thy pain.

Too eager caution shows some danger's near,
The bully's bluster proves the coward's fear;
His sober step the drunkard vainly tries,
And nymphs expose the failings they disguise.

First, whispering gossips were in parties seen;
Then louder Scandal walked the village-green;
Next babbling Folly told the growing ill,
And busy Malice dropp'd it at the mill.

"Go! to thy curse and mine," the Father said,
"Strife and confusion stalk around thy bed;
Want and a wailing brat thy portion be,
Plague to thy fondness, as thy fault to me; —
Where skulks the villain?" —
                              "On the ocean wide
My William seeks a portion for his bride." —
"Vain be his search! but, till the traitor come,

117

The higgler's cottage be thy future home;
There with his ancient shrew and care abide,
And hide thy head, — thy shame thou canst not hide."
    Day after day was pass'd in pains and grief;
Week follow'd week, — and still was no relief:
Her boy was born — no lads nor lasses came
To grace the rite or give the child a name;
Nor grave conceited nurse, of office proud,
Bore the young Christian roaring through the crowd:
In a small chamber was my office done,
Where blinks through papered panes the setting sun;
Where noisy sparrows, perched on penthouse near,
Chirp tuneless joy and mock the frequent tear;
Bats on their webby wings in darkness move,
And feebly shriek their melancholy love.
    No Sailor came; the months in terror fled!
Then news arrived — He fought, and he was DEAD!
    At the lone cottage Lucy lives, and still
Walks for her weekly pittance to the mill;
A mean seraglio there her father keeps,
Whose mirth insults her, as she stands and weeps;
And sees the plenty, while compell'd to stay,
Her father's pride, becomes his harlot's prey.
    Throughout the lanes she glides, at evening's close,
And softly lulls her infant to repose;
Then sits and gazes, but with viewless look,
As gilds the moon the rippling of the brook;
And sings her vespers, but in voice so low,
She hears their murmurs as the waters flow:
And she too murmurs and begins to find
The solemn wanderings of a wounded mind:
Visions of terror, views of wo succeed,
The mind's impatience, to the body's need;
By turns to that, by turns to this a prey,
She knows what reason yields, and dreads
                        what madness may.

George Crabbe

THE HUNCHBACK IN THE PARK

The hunchback in the park
A solitary mister
Propped between trees and water
From the opening of the garden lock
That lets the trees and water enter
Until the Sunday sombre bell at dark

Eating bread from a newspaper
Drinking water from the chained cup
That the children filled with gravel
In the fountain basin where I sailed my ship
Slept at night in a dog kennel
But nobody chained him up.

Like the park birds he came early
Like the water he sat down
And Mister they called Hey mister
The truant boys from the town
Running when he had heard them clearly
On out of sound

Past lake and rockery
Laughing when he shook his paper
Hunchbacked in mockery
Through the loud zoo of the willow groves
Dodging the park keeper
With his stick that picked up leaves.

And the old dog sleeper
Alone between nurses and swans
While the boys among willows
Made the tigers jump out of their eyes
To roar on the rockery stones
And the groves were blue with sailors

Made all day until bell time
A woman figure without fault
Straight as a young elm
Straight and tall from his crooked bones
That she might stand in the night
After the locks and chains

All night in the unmade park
After the railings and shrubberies
The birds the grass the trees the lake
And the wild boys innocent as strawberries
Had followed the hunchback
To his kennel in the dark.

Dylan Thomas

From *A PORTRAIT OF THE ARTIST AS A YOUNG MAN*

– Last and crowning torture of all the tortures of that awful
place is the eternity of hell. Eternity! O, dread and dire word.
Eternity! What mind of man can understand it? And remember,
it is an eternity of pain. Even though the pains of hell were not so
terrible as they are, yet they would become infinite, as they are
destined to last for ever. But while they are everlasting they are at
the same time, as you know, intolerably intense, unbearably
extensive. To bear even the sting of an insect for all eternity
would be a dreadful torment. What must it be, then, to bear the
manifold tortures of hell for ever? For ever! For all eternity!
Not for a year or for an age but for ever. Try to imagine the awful
meaning of this. You have often seen the sand on the seashore.
How fine are its tiny grains! And how many of those tiny little
grains go to make up the small handful which a child grasps in its
play. Now imagine a mountain of that sand, a million miles high,
reaching from the earth to the farthest heavens, and a million miles
broad, extending to remotest space, and a million miles in thickness; and imagine such an enormous mass of countless particles of
sand multiplied as often as there are leaves in the forest, drops of
water in the mighty ocean, feathers on birds, scales on fish, hairs
on animals, atoms in the vast expanse of the air: and imagine that
at the end of every million years a little bird came to that
mountain and carried away in its beak a tiny grain of that sand.
How many millions upon millions of centuries would pass before
that bird had carried away even a square foot of that mountain,
how many eons upon eons of ages before it had carried away all?
Yet at the end of that immense stretch of time not even one
instant of eternity could be said to have ended. At the end of all

those billions and trillions of years eternity would have scarcely begun. And if that mountain rose again after it had been all carried away, and if the bird came again and carried it all away again grain by grain, and if it so rose and sank as many times as there are stars in the sky, atoms in the air, drops of water in the sea, leaves on the trees, feathers upon birds, scales upon fish, hairs upon animals, at the end of all those innumerable risings and sinkings of that immeasurably vast mountain not one single instant of eternity could be said to have ended; even then, at the end of such a period, after that eon of time the mere thought of which makes our very brain reel dizzily, eternity would scarcely have begun.

James Joyce

What a terrifying piece of writing! And how it makes one remember the nightmares one had as a child, thinking about infinity and space. But the horror of it will not get over if you just go for its size — the horror of it is in its detail.

During the passages, to begin with, be conscious of the sweep of your inflections. Notice, for instance, if you start a new thought with a different note, or whether you tend to start it on the same note as you finished the previous sentence. You should get the sense of your voice moving on, that there is something further to come, and this involves keeping us in suspense. Lift the important points — particularly names, when they are mentioned for the first time.

Minor tone

Just a word here about what we call minor tone. Some people, when they speak, never seem to quite resolve their inflections — i.e., take them back to their key note, and the inflections go up and down in half-tones — often the result is complaining, and it is always irritating as it never seems quite finished and so does not satisfy the ear. It is rather like playing the second to last chord of a piece of music, and not finishing with the last chord — it leaves you stranded in mid-air. It is difficult to detect this in yourself, and I think you have to work on it with a tape recorder, for you have to hear it and then tally it with what you think you are doing, for there is usually that gap between what you think you are doing and what you actually are doing.

Through the kind of material there is in the book, and through finding a good variety of your own, you will learn to manipulate language and make your voice malleable so that it meets the demands of the material. Of course, when you are speaking on your own subject this is different as you have the benefit of your own authenticity — the conviction and enthusiasm you have for the subject. Use the exercises to find the extra variety you need.

Other material which is marvellous to use: all the Dylan Thomas short stories, the short stories of James Joyce, Katherine Mansfield, E. M. Forster. The poems and stories of D. H. Lawrence, John Betjeman's poetry, particularly a poem called *Beside the Seaside,* any Shaw prose or extracts from his plays. These are just suggestions, but most poetry is excellent, and all good prose.

9
Your Voice in Action

Now we have to gather all we have learnt and see how this works in the context of your own particular situation.

I think that no-one has ever come to me for voice lessons, be it politician, lecturer, teacher, priest or lawyer, but that, with all the exercises done, it comes down, in the end, to the simple point of how much you trust yourself and the value of what you are saying. It is always interesting to notice that people who are totally committed to what they are saying are so single-minded that they forget themselves and become part of what they are saying. I am thinking of people like Jimmy Read, who, one feels, is so politically committed that the thought of being nervous does not occur, or someone like Mohammed Ali. This is, I suspect, a rare gift and it is not the way through for most people. In any case, you should never be afraid of self-doubt, for questioning ourselves is the way we grow. But certainly, in the end, we have to find the trust and conviction, and if you are, in a sense, with the moment, and take the moment as it comes, you will find that. I think these words of T. S. Eliot, from *East Coker,* are good to digest:

> There is, it seems to us,
> At best, only a limited value
> In the knowledge derived from experience.
> The knowledge imposes a pattern, and falsifies,
> For the pattern is new in every moment
> And every moment is a new and shocking
> Valuation of all we have been.

It puts everything into perspective in the fact that each moment is different and we must use it.

All the exercises we have done will, I hope, help you to find a sense of unity so that you are behind and with everything you are saying. The exercises for being free help because they make you take time to be aware of yourself, and so be in tune with what is going on round you. Breathing correctly helps because it gives you a sense of your own weight and solidity, as a person and in your voice. The exercises for verbal muscularity help because they make your speech more positive, and when the speech is positive it helps to clarify your thought, because the commitment to your thought is greater. And it is good to be able to call on a certain range and variety for then you are confident in your ability to keep interest — though the reason for the interest must come out of what you are saying.

We have now covered all the technical ground and should have answered most of the questions. If your need is to make your voice feel better in an ordinary social context, certainly there is little more to say, except practise, read aloud as much as you can so you achieve a vocal freedom, take your time in conversation, and do not be afraid to allow silence. I think there is a common tendency to feel that if there is a silence in conversation it is your fault and you have some-how failed. This is not true at all, but if you become upset by it then you will not be able to think and you will become paralyzed by the situation. If you are calm and wait, something will come to your mind, it is as simple as that. If you feel you have an uneducated background, this is not important, because your experience may be richer than that of someone who is able to fill silence with trivia. The important thing is to value yourself.

Speaking in public

There are two general things I want to say about this, which pertain to any public situation.

1 About acoustics. There are no rules you can give on this, because each place in which you speak is different — and if it is a large space it is bound to have certain dead spots — but there are a few pointers. In a theatre, for instance, there is usually a dead spot in the back of the stalls, under the circle — often the first circle is quite difficult too — whereas the upper circle — 'the gods' — can be very good for sound, as the stage itself acts as a sounding board and throws the sound upwards. It depends on the kind of stage too, whether it is open and thrust forward, or proscenium. There are always difficult places for sound in any theatre, and actors become aware of this through experience. I have already said that churches are difficult, because of the predominance of stone in the building, which amplifies all the resonance — therefore it is the vowel sounds that are amplified, so the answer here is to increase the power of the consonant, but not to increase the volume. There is usually a place where you should pitch it to, or focus on, for the best result, but that you can only find by trying it out — you have to get somebody to listen to you in different parts of the building and tell you what the results are. Try focussing on different places, speak directly to each place, and find out which place makes the voice carry and which

does not.

Always bear in mind that the floor acts as a sounding board, so that when you focus on a fixed point it should always be near the floor — that is, if you throw your voice down, then the floor can act as a sounding board and bounce it up. This does not mean that you have to look down, you simply focus it down, along the floor. I remember, years ago, trying out my voice in the Albert Hall and learning something about this. If I stood on the stage part (where the orchestra sits) and simply threw the voice out in front towards the boxes, as loudly as I could, it got totally lost and one could not distinguish words at all. But if I focussed the voice down, onto the middle round part, where chairs are put for concerts, and pitched it to about the fourth row of those chairs, the voice and words carried easily with much less volume. So each place has a different answer, and you have to discover it for yourself — though do remember that it is the energy in the consonants that makes the words carry. You will find that the more experience you have, the more you will be able to sense what works and what does not. The pointers are: consonants, and use the floor.

If the building has microphones, then it is a matter of coming to terms with them. They will work differently in each place — but again it is consonants not volume that are important. I do not mean be explosive with the consonants — that can be confusing — I mean use their weight and allow the vibrations and friction to impinge.

2   The second point is very important — and not technical as such. It is the awareness of the value of pauses. Already I have said that pauses are part of giving variety to speech, but they are much more than that.

To begin with, the listener needs a certain number of pauses to be able to take in and digest what you are saying — this you have to sense. When listening we need moments of rest, as it were, to give us time to receive. Try to recognize this need. Secondly, and just as important, you need those moments of rest so that you can receive back from your audience, and become sensitive and attuned to them. They are valuable to you. Thirdly, to pause gives you energy, because you find you can collect energy from your audience, and, what is more, if you take time to pause, you allow yourself time to reach down inside for your own energy, and for what you have to give. I believe very strongly that we know things in our sub-conscious before that knowledge reaches our conscious mind — i.e., we make up our mind in our stomach, as it were, before we rationalize things mentally, so that if we take time to listen for our subconscious, our intuition, what comes out will be the richer. Pauses are also valuable in that they have the effect of drawing people to listen — if people have to wait sometimes for what you have to say then they listen more acutely. This is really a technical thing, a trick of the trade you could call it, and, I think, valid so long as you know why you are doing it — but use it with discretion! Lastly, when you do take these moments off and come to rest, you find that you start the new thought with a fresh impulse, and so are more likely to use new notes and keep the impetus going through your speaking. Pauses are valuable, providing you use them with honesty.

I think we have covered all the points that are relevant. I know you will get very valuable insights into dealing with audiences and making contact with them from the firsthand knowledge of those who are contributing to the book. They are of infinite value.

There are just one or two comments I would like to make regarding the differing needs of different jobs or professions — though, of course, you know those needs best, and so will be able to judge accordingly.

In Business

1   If you are using your voice a lot in business situations — either at conferences and congresses, or in a less public way, simply in selling your product — the important thing to remember is not to over-pressurize and not to be over-emphatic, for this is not always the right way to get confidence. Quiet authority has great value. This is a difficult area to talk about, because your belief in what you are saying is of paramount importance, and of course there are times when you have to be politic, but do listen to what others have to say and allow yourself time to take it in so that you can take up those points and use them. Also, when presenting points at a meeting, it is the homework that you have done on your facts that gives you security, and enables you to present them clearly and with logical progression. Any indication of muddle or lack of clarity is really damaging. Therefore good preparation is the most important thing to do — then you can allow the technical means that you will have found to carry you. So, make your points clearly but not dog-matically, know your objective and unfold the content in logical stages so that it can be taken in easily.

In Politics

2   The same also applies to anyone making a more public kind of address, political or otherwise. If you are in that kind of situation you will only be there because of your enthusiasm for the subject, so

allow that enthusiasm to carry, yet keep cool enough to make your points logically. Do not be afraid or ashamed of using full notes, for they keep you on a direct track. Sometimes you can fool yourself by thinking that your enthusiasm gives you the right to ramble and get side-tracked — this is a dangerous thing. And, as you will be well aware, it is important to leave your audience wanting more. Brevity always comes out on your side! And all humour is a bonus, providing it is your own humour and comes out of your particular attitude and observation. Of course, to be able to use humour, and answer back quickly if heckled only comes with experience and assurance, and you cannot force it. I think it is very valuable when addressing a large audience to keep this person-to-person angle well in mind. The trap that so many politicians, for instance, fall into, is in getting a kind of generalized attitude, which results in a generalized kind of rhetorical 'noise' — we all know this kind of political haranguing, it has a special sound and is not particular to the person. There are, of course, certain political points that you have to put over, but the simpler you can be — and presumably you would not be saying them unless you believed in them — the more they will impinge and persuade. It is all too easy to talk in clichés, and what is politics anyway if not of direct and intimate concern to each person. The danger is always to try to give more significance to a point than is actually valid — to bloat it, in other words. It actually makes the listener very cynical. Be accurate with the words you choose.

Teaching Situations

3   Teachers seem to me in a particular class of their own. Lecturers do not have anywhere near the same kind of problems of discipline, though I know they have to keep interest, so that what they need is variety and clarity and to allow their own human experience to influence how they put their subject — their own warmth and generosity matters very much. But teachers in schools are under a very particular pressure, and it is interesting that nearly all the teachers I have met have always complained of vocal fatigue, and that their voice goes at the end of the day. Now all the exercises in relaxation and breathing are the technical answers, and you cannot find better. But I think you also have to recognize the stress of the classroom situation, which is to some degree an emotional one, so that very often the vocal fatigue, I have noticed, shows signs of emotional fatigue. It is difficult for me to explain, except that I know I can always tell the difference between vocal fatigue which is simple tiredness, and vocal fatigue which has a certain emotional pressure contributing to it. Teachers are very aware of the demand

for attention that thirty or more individuals need and are in some way asking for. It is not only the fact of reaching thirty people with clarity of speech, it is answering their particular needs as individuals, and the awful awareness that if you do not make some kind of personal contact, particular to each one, much of what you say will have little meaning. It really is a difficult situation. The pressure is in the fact that a teacher has to keep order, his success in societal terms depends very much on whether he keeps good discipline, and yet the very nature of being a good teacher is the desire to share on a personal basis, and the sharing of knowledge in human terms, which is not necessarily conducive to good discipline in the accepted sense. Only a small percentage of teachers come to a satisfactory balance. This is such a personal matter that one cannot give advice generally, all one can do is say, make your voice as strong as it can be so that you can rely on it, and then share your experience as much as you can. Moments of silence are very valuable indeed in a teaching situation, for they make the student curious about what you may be thinking, and he will therefore regard this with value. Again, it is a matter of valuing what you have to give.

Churchmen and Preaching

4   As I have already said, clergymen and priests often have acoustic problems, but those I have dealt with, and I think because their work is so constant they have the benefit of gaining experience quite quickly, and also are well prepared for it during their training and, I think, they are well-equipped to deal with their own situations. However, I think sometimes what happens when they become quite experienced is that they rely on certain attitudes, and do not always think afresh each time they are preaching or speaking. This tends to result in a sort of manner, which often signals a certain paternal attitude, a kind of over-understanding, and easily becomes a general manner and not a particular point of view. I am sure it is a difficult job, in that it has to do with reassurance and continually answering the same kind of spiritual questions. It is just that it is so important to keep the thought fresh each time. This kind of generalized attitude also creeps into reading the Bible very often, and one has to be continually on one's guard about this, so that each time one reads it, it is fresh — for in fact it is. Each time you read it, it will mean something slightly different because of fresh experience and the different moment in time. The importance is really being with the moment, and reading for this moment.

5   Broadcasting and television are something for which really there
are no rules, simply because it is the immediacy of the communication which matters, and some people have the gift for this and some
do not. I think it is something that you either have naturally or not
at all, not something you can learn. For even if you play a serious
rôle in television – i.e., dealing with news and documentary material,
you either come alive on the screen or you do not – that is just a fact
and there is nothing you can do about it. However serious you are being,
there must also be something of the showman in you to want to put
it across by this means, so that we are not only informed by you, but
to some degree entertained. We are also entertained by someone who
has the reputation of being bad-tempered and rude – the entertain-
ment value is in the suspense as to whether the person will be rude or
lose his temper – what we do not like is to be bored – that is the
cardinal sin. We like eccentricity, and there can be no rules or advice
about that, for it is a personal commodity which is part of the
individual and cannot be planned – though it can be exploited! The
important thing is to relax and be yourself, and do not over-pressurize
– this is something that I do think happens to sports commentators
in particular, a kind of over-emphasis of the immediacy of the
situation. Apart from that, you can only be particularly alive and
curious about what gets through to other people and the impression
you make, and adjust accordingly. I always find it interesting to
notice that some personalities come over incredibly well on radio,
yet when you see them they are disappointing – it also happens the
reverse way round. Just as the image you have of somebody when
you talk to them on the telephone may differ greatly from their
appearance in everyday life. This happens very much with pop
singers too, or pop groups – some are better performers than
musicians, and with some the enjoyment goes a little when you see
them. The lucky ones are those who are good at both. Success in
radio or television is very often accidental, but once it happens you
have to use it and make it grow.

6   I think my views, as regards parents influencing the way children
speak, are probably quite clear from the beginning pages of the book.
It seems vital to me that children should be allowed to be articulate
and be given time to express thoughts and experiences, for they are
always interesting. Once you lose their desire to talk to you, you
lose contact. And it is later that they will suffer. Of course they
have maddening habits, and go through stages of being rude, or
feeling it is clever to swear etc., but they soon learn to give it its

proper value. You cannot stop them using slang, it is part of their growth, or falling in with other children who perhaps do not speak as well as you would like — again it is a stage, and if you can only listen without disapproval, it is a stage they will quickly get over. Unless there is any particular reason, like some sort of speech impediment, when, of course, they should see a therapist, I do not think they should be taught how to speak. At any rate, not until they are old enough to know the reason and appreciate its value. The important thing is to keep them talking. Children are easily discouraged.

Amateur Drama

7   My last section is for those who enjoy taking part in amateur theatre. All we have done so far in the book is valuable, but of course it can be taken further by studying as many and varied dramatic texts as possible, for the actor needs to be able to call on as much vocal variety and resource as he can.

The demands an actor makes on his voice are the most exacting of all, for he not only has to be true to himself, he has to explore the vocal possibilities of other characters saying words that are not his own. And one of the main problems of the actor is taking words off the printed page and absorbing them into his consciousness to such a degree that they become his own words — a process of osmosis. My first book *Voice and the Actor* goes a long way I think to help the actor explore his voice for the particular way in which he has to use it. It certainly came out of a long experience of teaching actors and being aware of their difficulties and needs.

The actor is much more vulnerable than most people would suppose, and needs a great deal of reassurance. As an artist he is unique in that he is using only himself — his body, his voice and his experience — to express and convey his particular form of art. The painter has his paints and brush, the musician has his music and his instrument, the dancer has certain formalized movements and a rhythmic structure as his discipline, the singer has the notes of music and particular ways of using resonance — but the actor has himself. Of course he has a text and a character to interpret, but the choices he can make for any one character are infinite, as anyone who has seen Hamlet played by a number of different actors will realize, and the depth of his interpretation will depend on his own emotional depth as a person, and how much of his own experience he brings to bear on it.

I suppose the actor's chief problem is one of size — the space he has to fill. For he has to be able to share an experience with a large number of people, who make up the audience, and yet keep the sense of intimacy which he is creating between himself and the other actors on the stage. Once he loses that sense of playing with his fellow actors, he will start to push vocally and lose any credibility and atmosphere which he has built up.

Much depends on the size of the character you are having to create — if you are in a modern play which is not very demanding it may be relatively easy to relate your own experience to this, but if you are playing in something with a certain depth, where the characters take you into an area which is outside your own experience, be it Pinter or Beckett, Shaw or Restoration comedy, Jacobean tragedy or Shakespeare, then the journey is a much more difficult one, and one which takes time to discover.

Firstly, never hurry that journey. The actor, being insecure as he so often is, always feels under a certain pressure to present something. The great danger, even for the professional actor, is to start presenting a character at the beginning of rehearsals — just to show he can. And once you start presenting a character you stop discovering things about it. It takes a certain confidence and a certain nerve to hold back at early rehearsals and wait for something to happen inside — an acquaintance with that character which should grow organically. Once you begin to know how that character reacts to different situations, how he feels, how he moves, then vocally you will begin to respond and the voice will begin to sound like the character. For you should never think in terms of 'putting on a voice', or finding a character voice — that will always be false — the voice must grow with the character and be the outward result of what you have discovered about that person. Different people go about this discovery in different ways. By reading all the books on acting, such as those by Stanislavski, you can lay your hands on, you will begin to realize the complexity of the process and how each person has to find their own way in. But what you can be quite clear about is that your discovery of a character must come through a search of yourself, finding the things in you which relate to the character, and this requires a great deal of honesty sometimes. For if you do not like certain aspects of the character, you have to find aspects of yourself which you perhaps do not like and try to see how they can bring you to a closer understanding of the character. I believe we can find all kinds of emotional responses in ourselves if we choose to be open and recognize them — of course we do not indulge those responses if they are harmful, but we can recognize them, and by doing so lead ourselves to an understanding of any character we wish to play.

How we get to the character, of course, is through the words he has to say. If you are playing a modern text much of the dialogue is concerned with covering up feelings, and so you have to look for the underlying motive, or drive, or action — whatever you like to call it. Beckett's characters, for instance, through a series of disconnected memories and images, build up a picture of a whole life. Whereas Shakespeare, at the other end of the scale, is a process of discovering the action in the word — the action is implicit in the word and the word is the action. You cannot take time off to feel when you are acting Shakespeare, for the feeling is in the word at that moment, and the words give you the scale or measure of that feeling. So much so that the rhythm of the writing alters as the emotional state of the character alters. Othello, for instance, at the beginning of the play speaks in lofty well-rounded phrases with splendid imagery, but as the play progresses, and the jealousy provoked by Iago begins to work, his speech becomes broken up and jerky, and when at last he cracks he talks in prose with the kind of debased imagery of animals that Iago uses naturally. It is fascinating to plot the emotional states of the characters in Shakespeare by the rhythm of their speeches and the kind of imagery they use.

So you can learn much and extend your range by taking speeches of one particular character in any good play — modern or classic — and finding out as much as you can about the character by the words he uses. Shakespeare is an unlimited source, the Jacobean dramatists like Webster and Middleton are also rich. The texts of Jacobean dramatists are really rewarding to tackle, they are extremely difficult, more so I think than Shakespeare in that the meaning is more difficult to grasp and make clear, and to speak it you have to clarify the meaning so that it is understandable, but you also have to allow the heightened language to take off and the images themselves to be wholly experienced. The language the characters use, and the imagery, are not our language and our imagery, therefore you have to become familiar with it so that it becomes authentic and credible on your tongue — this is not easy and takes a great effort of imagination to come to terms with.

All good comedy is useful too to work on — Shaw particularly, in that it is so verbal, and you have to believe totally in what you are saying. If, for one moment, you come outside the character and start thinking that what you are saying is funny, you are lost. It is only funny if you are absolutely with the thought and committed to what the character is saying. You can learn so much about rhythm and variety in studying any of the large parts in Shaw. But, of course, all good comedy depends on how much you believe in the reality of the situation. Restoration comedy is much more difficult in that it requires a considerable knowledge of the manners of the time, and is difficult to study on your own. But studying any of these plays has something to do with reaching out to characters and situations which are larger than ourselves, and this is always a good thing to do, for it enriches our experience and our imagination.

One most important thing to remember is always to go for the truth of the action, and never present an audience with a generalized kind of emotional quality. That is to say, if you are playing a tragic part, or a sad part, you as a character are not sad or tragic, and the audience does not want to be given a 'tragic' performance. Your situation may be tragic, but you as a character are not aware of this, you are too busy and too involved with the action. Hamlet does not know he is a tragic figure, he is behaving as his reason and feelings dictate – he is not acting tragedy, but he happens to be in a tragic situation. And if you present your audience with a tragic quality, what you are actually doing is being outside the character, making a comment on him, telling your audience that this is sad. The audience does not want to be told, they want to be allowed to come to their own conclusions out of the situation in which the character finds himself. What you are really doing is signalling to your audience that you understand and that you feel – in other words you are 'doing', not 'being'.

As an actor, when working in the context of a rehearsal or a performance, you have to be acutely sensitive to others you are working with. You have to listen, for the way they hand you their dialogue will influence and alter how you say your lines. Listening accurately is one of the most important things an actor has to learn, for how can you reply to someone on the stage unless you have fully heard what they have said. You have to be so prepared that you can react to the moment. And that is what voice exercises for the actor are about – to make his voice so alive and in tune, that it can respond to the instinct of the moment, and gather the energy from the other actors around him.

So, never come to do a part with a preconceived idea of what it should sound like, listen for what it has to tell you – for what the words say – and always respond to it afresh.

I hope that you have found the practical things in this book that you need to allow you to use your voice as completely as possible. It should be an enjoyable experience – for the picture will not be good unless you enjoy the painting of it – and the enjoyment also comes out of sharing the experience.

Summary of Exercises

When you feel you have a real familiarity with the exercises, and know their progression, you may find it useful to have a summary of them to work through, as a prompt or guide, so that you do not have to keep turning pages to find them. So I include the following summary.

Relaxation and Breathing

1   Lie on the floor, feeling the back as spread as possible –
         i.e., the shoulders and back widening and the head lengthen-
         ing out of the back. Do not get a feeling of sinking into the
         floor but rather of spreading over it.
         Feel the shoulders, neck and arms free, so the joints are easing
         away from each other and not pressed in.

2   Put your hands on the side of the ribs, where the rib cage is
         widest and:

a)   Breathe in – sigh out pushing all the air right out – wait until
         you feel the muscles between the ribs needing to move – then
         fill in again slowly feeling the ribs widening at the back and
         sides. Try not to lift the top of the chest. Repeat several
         times.

b)   Breathe in – then out slowly for 10 counts – being aware of the
         muscles between the ribs controlling the breath. Increase the
         count out to 15 and then to 20.

c)   Breathe in all the way round – put one hand on your
         diaphragm and sigh out from there several times, gently but
         firmly, to feel where the breath starts – then put a little
         sound to it on 'ER' – touching it off like a drum – then a
         more sustained sound on 'AH', 'AY' and 'I' – joining the
         breath to the sound.

d)   Breathe in so that the ribs are open – put one hand on the
         diaphragm – sigh out easily through an open throat – then
         fill in again and count to 6 aloud on that breath. Continue
         with a short piece of text you know, making sure you fill
         right down each time you breathe so that the breath starts
         the sound. Root the sound to the breath.
         Keep checking that the shoulders and neck are free.

3   Get into a good position, either sitting or standing – back
         widening and lengthening.

134

Drop forward and lift slowly, feeling the muscles in the back of
the neck pulling up.
Drop back and lift.
Drop to the sides and stretch and lift.
Roll round as fully as possible.
Tense slightly back — relax and feel the difference.
Nod gently from an upright position, feeling the muscles in the
back of the neck free.
A very small roll round to get the sensation of freedom of
movement — so the head may be still but not fixed.

Shoulders

Lift and drop gently, let them go that extra bit.
Notice what it feels like when they are released.
4 a) With your hands behind your head — as relaxed as possible —
breathe in and sigh right out — to the last little bit — wait until
the ribs need to move — then let the ribs widen and fill in.
Repeat two or three times only. This opens the chest.
  b) Hands down, or on the side of your ribs — breathe in fully and
out slowly for 10, 15 and 20 counts — being aware of the
muscles between the ribs controlling the breath.
  c) Breathe in and sigh out from the diaphragm on 'ER' feeling the
breath and sound together. Then on a more sustained vowel
'AH', 'AY' and 'I'. When you feel the sound is rooted down,
speak some text on that breath.

Always keep the upper chest, neck and shoulders free.
When speaking your text, reach down to the diaphragm for the
sound, so that you get a sense of the tone coming unhindered from
there, then the chest can contribute to the resonance. The throat
should feel entirely free.
The important thing is to feel the muscles working — i.e., the
muscles between the ribs, and the diaphragm — because it is the
muscular tone that gives the vocal tone substance. One, of course,
exaggerates the movement of the muscles in exercise simply to be
aware of them. Ultimately, the breathing should be economical and
smooth, but the extra energy needed to project — to enable you to
keep intimacy and subtlety and yet be large enough — should come
from this whole use of the voice.

5   *Muscularity*

With and without bone-prop, exercise the tongue and lip muscles;

Tongue tip

a)

la	la	la	la
lala	lala	lala	lala
lalala	lalala	lalala	lah

make the tongue tip drop to the bottom each time.

b)

tetete	tetete	tetete	tah
dedede	dedede	dedede	dah
nenene	nenene	nenene	nah

Back of tongue

a)

kekeke	kekeke	kekeke	kah
gegege	gegege	gegege	gah

b)

kekeke	tetete
gegege	dedede

Lips

a)

pepepe	pepepe	pepepe	pah
bebebe	bebebe	bebebe	bah
mememe	mememe	mememe	mah

b)   mememe   nenene — keep this clear of the nose.

In exercise, press the tongue and the lip muscles hard, so you become aware of them — they also contribute to the resonance and give it dimension.

Exercise the lips with the following vowels:

AH	OO		
AH	AW	OO	
AH	AW	OO	OW
MAH	MAW	MOO	MOW
PAH	PAW	POO	POW
BAH	BAW	BOO	BOW

Exercise the front part of the blade of the tongue with the
following vowels, keeping the back of the tongue relaxed:

AH	EE		
AH	AY	EE	
AH	AY	EE	I
LAH	LAY	LEE	LI
TAH	TAY	TEE	TI
DAH	DAY	DEE	DI
NAH	NAY	NEE	NI

Feel the front of the tongue arching upwards.

EAR	AIR
LEAR	LAIR
TEAR	TAIR
DEAR	DAIR
NEAR	NAIR

Feel the tongue moving down.

Say: 'Vvvvvvvvvv' and 'Zzzzzzz' several times holding
on to the consonant and feeling the vibration on the
lips and tongue.

In all these exercises, rapidity is not important, it is the firmness of
the muscular movement which is essential, and the awareness of
the vibration on the consonant, because the tone must come to
where the words are formed. It is this muscular firmness which
makes the words carry and which is the physical part of projection. The voice should come unhindered from the diaphragm to
be formed into words and given a 'send-off' by the lips and
tongue. It should then be effortless and have no strain on the
throat.

137

6   *To open the throat:*

a)   Drop the jaw and feel the tongue and neck quite relaxed and open. Make the muscles in the back of the tongue and palate work by saying: 'gegege' very hard, pushing the tongue up to the back of the palate, feeling them both tensed. Then drop the tongue and the palate and feel them relaxed. So you are aware of both the tension and the relaxation.

b)   Repeat in this way:

gegege   with the back of the palate and tongue tensed.
gegege   with the palate and tongue dropped.

Hear the difference in sound.

gegege   tense
gegege   relaxed
AH   dropped and open

Then with relaxed tongue and palate:

gegege   AH
gegege   AY
gegege   I

Keep the consonants firm and the vowels open.

c)   Then, using plenty of breath, sing out on 'AY' and 'I', making sure the sound is starting at the diaphragm.
Repeat this, swinging down from side to side with your arms and head, making sure the head drops completely each time.

7   Stand ordinarily, and work on a piece of text, combining the result of all the exercises – i.e., breathing, relaxation and muscularity.

Ultimately, what makes the voice particular, is the mental-physical tie-up – i.e., that the voice is free and responsive enough to reflect what you think and feel. It must be as interesting as what you have to communicate. It should always be able to surprise us. Its job is to make us remark on what is remarkable.

10
Speakers on Speaking

We have covered all the aspects of using the voice and related them to different situations – size of audience, space, etc. We have discovered how to relax, how to breathe, how to speak with clarity and to sound as interesting as possible – all the things which enable you to project with ease and so make you feel generally confident. Yet, although all this helps, it still does not answer completely the specific problem of getting up and facing people, of putting your own ideas across in your own words – whether it be a short after-dinner speech of welcome or thanks, taking part in a debate, or a more formal kind of speech in which you are putting across serious ideas – in a way I think the latter is the easiest in that the subject and content are more specific.

Of course, in the end it is up to you – it is your personality and the words you choose which get across your message. If you did not have something to say, or were not the right person for the occasion, you would, presumably, not be there. The fact that you have something you want to say, which you believe has value and makes a contribution to the situation, is why you are there – this is a simple thing to say, but in fact it is the anchor which, more than anything, gives you confidence. To many people speaking in public is a hurdle, but overcoming this hurdle really comes down to what I said in the last chapter – it is to do with trusting yourself, committing yourself wholly to what you are saying, and believing in your right to be there.

I thought that the most helpful thing to do would be to speak to one or two people who are known to be in the top rank of speakers, and get their views on how they approach speaking in public, any technical hints they may have, and generally their attitude to an audience. And though I think the things they have said all affirm what we have already found out, by an individual image or vivid turn of phrase, each one of them has illuminated something about the subject, and so clarified the process and made it more accessible. So often it is an image or phrase which sticks in your mind which actually sparks you off into being able to do something really well – so who better to ask than those with first-hand experience.

In the conversations I had with each of the contributors, I asked them basically the same questions, though, because they were fundamentally conversations, the questions did not come out formally or in the same order. I think it is essentially this informality – the tangents they go off on and the anecdotes they tell – which informs us, and, what is even more important, makes us aware of their very human attitude towards their business – their skill.

Starting with the question of nervousness, which is a fundamental one for us, I asked each one of them if they had ever been particularly nervous, and if so, how they had dealt with it, and also if any particular situation made them uneasy now. Now all of them are gifted speakers, certainly without problems about being articulate, though that may be from enthusiasm for, and curiosity about, what they have to say, and I suspect that none of them have been really nervous – I mean to the point of being paralysed by a situation. However, they all had very practical things to say on how to overcome nerves – by practice, good preparation and attitude of mind.

I then asked how they went about preparing a speech – the technical matter of whether they wrote it out in full, used notes or headlines, or had no notes at all. This, of course, is where they varied most, and where each varied with the occasion also. Clearly this is a matter of individual choice, and what makes you most comfortable. I suspect that at the beginning the fuller your notes are the better and, as you become practised, so you will find out what suits you best. However, what they are all quite clear about is that there is skill in presenting a speech. If you have the complete transcript of your speech and you read it, then you must practise reading so that you can look at your transcript without shifting focus from your audience down onto your paper – this is not always an easy thing to do. It is important that the audience feel that they are the centre of your attention, and that you are comfortable with them – if your attention is divided and you get flustered between your notes and them you will destroy their confidence in you, and lose your rapport with them. It is important to realise that this is something that you can become skilled in doing. Again, if you read from notes or headlines, make yourself absolutely familiar with them, know how to handle them, so that you can use them without losing contact with your audience. This involves very simple commonsense things like knowing where to place them so that you can see them easily, which has to do with your eyesight and whether you are short or long sighted. In other words, know how to make yourself comfortable.

I asked them what guidelines they gave themselves when it came to preparing a speech, and here they each had vivid things to say. Most important is their insistence that, whether you are preparing a speech, or gathering your thoughts to take part in a debate or conference situation, you must be quite clear about your ideas, have one or two points that you want to make – not more – make them clearly, and restate them if necessary. The important thing being not how much you get over, but the clarity with which you get it over.

The most vivid and personal responses came when I asked them how they gauged an audience and made contact with it. As you would expect, it was obvious that each one got tremendous pleasure and stimulus from speaking to an audience – it was something they liked doing. There is the entertainer in them all. They enjoy engaging the interest of an audience by employing their own particular brand of humour, by a sense of timing, by being able to keep their listeners in suspense, by shock tactics – by a sense of drama in fact. They enjoy the occasion, and are able to use these tactics and play with their audience, not in an insincere or false way, simply so that they can keep the interest of their audience to make what is serious about their speech the more telling. And of course we as an audience love it, because we like to be entertained and we also always appreciate seeing something done skilfully – this is always pleasurable. Now of course it takes experience to do this, for if a speaker has a reputation, then the audience turns up with a sense of expectation – like going to hear a favourite comedian – and the speaker has those ready made vibrations to play with. This also requires skill, because you have to live up to that reputation no matter how you may feel – headache, cold, whatever. The point I want to make is that you have to start out sensibly, being objective about yourself, because you cannot start manipulating speeches in this way until you have a certain basic security, and until you have won the respect of your audience – you have to earn the right to do it. What we learn from this, therefore, is that it is important to get as much experience as possible in speaking and debating. As Lord Mancroft says, join local debating societies, find out by practical experience what you can do, how to debate, how to use what other people say and turn it to your own advantage, and you will begin to enjoy it as a skill. For it is only by confidence and security that you will have the nerve to pause and feel the response of your audience – listen for their vibrations – it is only by confidence that you will be able to develop your own style, bring your own humour, your own warmth, and your own attitude to life, to bear on what you

141

are saying at each moment.

Obviously some people do have a head start in that they have a gift for speaking well — as Dr Stockwood says, comparatively few people compel interest naturally — it is a rare gift. But we all have the potential ability to put across what we have to say clearly and accurately, and if what we have to say is interesting, then it will be so. It is a matter of sharing your knowledge and experience.

I also asked them if their voices became strained and, if so, whether they did any voice exercises or consciously relaxed. Also, I was interested in whether they were encouraged to speak when they were young — Lord Mancroft has something interesting to say on that — and also whether they had been influenced by anyone in particular.

Here are some of the things they said. Although a lot of what they say is in common with each other, the way they describe their own particular ways of contacting an audience is so totally individual, and gives flashes of insight into them as people and the way they work — in other words, the language they use. It makes the whole business of speaking in public appear an exciting and stimulating challenge. And this at all levels of communication — light after-dinner speech or learned tract.

Lord Mancroft

'I am surprised that anyone is willing to talk about how they make speeches — it is like giving away trade secrets!' This was the marvellous opening remark from Lord Mancroft when I went to talk to him. As I talked to each of the speakers I realized how pertinent that remark was, for it became more and more apparent that each one I talked to had an absolutely objective awareness of his own skill in front of an audience, which was every bit as cunning and adaptable as that of a variety entertainer.

He then went on to tell me a fascinating story about Churchill, when he was the guest of honour at a dinner at which Lord Mancroft was also speaking. It happened to be the night when the news of the war in Korea broke, so that Churchill switched from his prepared light-hearted speech to one which was more appropriate to the moment. Lord Mancroft's own speech, which came after Churchill's, was drowned by the noise of pressmen grabbing for the telephone. And Lord Mancroft goes on: 'Winston very kindly sent for me and said "I am sorry I did not hear a word you said, may I see your notes." And I said: "Mr Churchill, I only use three or four very short lines", and he said: "I have mine almost verbatim, look at mine." Not only was it almost verbatim, but it was phrased and parsed, and marked *rallentando* and so on. I noticed with astonishment the care he went to to get his voice right, the breathing right and where the emphasis should be.'

I think it is interesting to know that someone who was as brilliant as Churchill in speaking, should be so aware of the technical means of communicating what he wanted – very much like an actor in fact, who, in preparing one of the major speeches in a classical drama, has to know where his climaxes are, what is important and what can be thrown away, how to build and shape the speech so that it will be clear to his audience. Certainly Churchill was very aware of the emotive power of his speaking.

I wanted in particular to find out from Lord Mancroft how important he felt good speaking was to the business man in ordinary everyday affairs. He was very firm about the value of clear thinking, and therefore clear speaking, in business, and stressed that you can only get someone's confidence if you are articulate and speak with authority. 'If you see doubt on a man's face,' he said, 'you say, "well I haven't got that over to you clearly, let me try again" – or – "you don't agree with me, do you Jack, what's worrying you".' He stressed that you should never be afraid to go back over a point.

He went on: 'I always encourage the younger members of my staff to think about public speaking. It is part of their training at an early stage, certainly on the sales and operational side. At a very early stage they should join things like their local Rotary Club or their local Chamber of Commerce and learn to speak in debate. It is part of the equipment of any senior executive to put over the case of his business in as convincing and authoritative a way as he possibly can. The man who can do that really well has half sold his product. The man who does it badly and dithers, and "ums" and "ers" has put off the other side straight away. They think he is incompetent and has no clear thought, and cannot make up his mind. You will find that there are very few people who are really efficient leaders in business or politics or charity who are not really articulate.'

He was very interesting about his own preparation, and particularly of how his father encouraged him from a very early age to consciously present his thoughts and ideas in a coherent and balanced way – to speak with care and thought. He would come back from a walk, or having been out somewhere, anxious to tell his father what he had been doing and what he had seen, and his father would say: 'Just a minute, not too fast. Think it out carefully, and by the way stand on that stool and begin by saying "Ladies and Gentlemen".' So that he got into the habit very young of thinking over what he was going to tell his father, and trying to say it in a way that would amuse and interest him. This was a remarkable thing to do. He also said of his father: 'He was a Member of Parliament himself, and he was a very good speaker. He had a completely different style from most people, a very conversational style, but he could think very quickly on his feet.'

About his own preparation he said: 'I prepare speeches certainly, but I do not have full notes — I am so shortsighted I cannot see without spectacles. I just have headlines to show me the shape of the speech, or, if there is a particular figure I want to mention, or a quotation, then I pick up my notes firmly in my hand and read them.

'You always should be clear in your mind about what you are going to say — you must be certain how you are going to begin and how you are going to end. You must leave space in a speech to reply to some pleasant remark — I am talking of the after-dinner speech now. You have always got to leave space to take up somebody else's point. The most difficult speeches to make are those at mixed dinners — mixed is usually social and they do not want to listen to you yapping. The vaguer the subject the more difficult it is to compose. Now if you asked me to speak tonight to a male audience on the subject of the Tote or gambling, on which I am well-versed, that would be comparatively easy, the subject is at my finger-tips.'

He referred to his father again: 'It was he who told me you must marshal your thoughts tidily in a correct order, and not end up with things like "don't you know" or "kind of" — get your sentences correctly constructed and as accurate as you possibly can. Try and use words that will keep people's attention — when you have an arresting thought, put it into arresting words.'

About audiences and speakers he said: 'What is surprising is how one audience can look exactly the same as another and be totally different. A joke that went down with Audience A extremely well, can fall flat as a pancake with Audience B. Some speakers can irritate you beyond endurance. When someone asked him how he enjoyed an evening, Bernard Shaw said: "I enjoyed myself — that's about the only thing I did enjoy".'

To sum up, he said: 'A speech must have a form. The old dictum — tell them what you are going to say, say it, tell them what you have said. In other words, make certain at the beginning they know very quickly what you are going to talk about, go into it as quickly as you can, then have your reasoning in the middle, so they know why you want them to believe what you are telling them, then sum up at the end and make certain they have got the point. And do not put too many points in one speech — do not cram too much in.'

Marjorie Proops

As you might expect, Marjorie Proops's understanding of the
difficulties that people have in communicating with each other was so
perceptive, that we talked more about that than the business of
speaking in public, although she has much first-hand experience of
that.

Because her job is totally to do with people's relationships to each
other, she gets asked a lot for advice on how to speak – sometimes
at a very personal level. She told me one sad story: 'I had a letter
from a woman once, who said that after being married for a long
time happily, she and her husband had had a bad row, and he told
her he could not stand her voice any longer. I did not know what
to say. But finally I advised her to get a tape recorder and leave it on
for some time and listen – I do not know whether that helped.' I
know that that story is not to do with speaking in public, but it does
highlight so tangibly how little we know about the impressions we
make on other people, and that if we could be clearer about this and
willing to make adjustments, we would make better contact with other
people. Of course, this was a unique case, but even so there is something we can learn from it.

We talked also of the value of silence when we are speaking to
other people. And she told me another story, which again is not
specifically to do with public speaking, but in its way it is relevant.
She told me how, when she was doing a series of interviews for
television about marriage, she was interviewing a woman in a
launderette who was doing the family wash. She had asked her two
or three questions which the woman had answered quite normally,
and she was in the middle of saying something when she stopped,
and there was a long pause, and Marjorie Proops did not know whether
to come in or not, for the pause was going on too long really for a
television programme, but she hung on, and then, quite suddenly, the
woman spoke and it all poured out – her whole story, about her
husband, her family, her unhappiness, etc., and Miss Proops said:
'I was tempted to break the silence, but I did not. If I had done, I
would have missed all that story.' She went on to say that as a piece
of reporting it was too personal actually to be made public, but that
if we do not wait sometimes for what people have to say we can miss
so very much.

On the more practical side of speaking to an audience, I asked her
whether she got nervous: 'I am nervous sometimes, especially when
I am called on suddenly, like at a big lunch here at work, where I
know everyone, perhaps on the occasion of someone leaving –
people say, "Come on, Marje, say something." I am always nervous

in front of friends. I was very fortunate in my early youth in that I trained as a singer. I won the all-England contralto contest when I was fourteen, out of ninety-three finalists, singing *O rest in the Lord.* Voice production, more than anything, gave me confidence.'

About the specific subject of women speaking in public she had a good deal to say, particularly as she gets so many letters asking for help in making an after-dinner speech. 'If a professional woman knows her subject, for example a gynaecologist, she can speak on her subject as well as a man. But it is quite a different matter for the poor lady wife of the worshipful master at a masonic ladies' night when she has to reply to a toast — many women find this very difficult. As a matter of fact lots of women write in to me asking what to say. I have the beginning of a speech ready prepared to start them off.'

MASONIC LADIES' NIGHT SPEECH

Someone once mentioned that it is every woman's secret dream to become a mistress. I don't know about the other ladies here tonight, but ever since my husband became a Freemason, it has been my secret dream to stand up here as his mistress on this great occasion.

It's probably the one and only time I'll ever be a mistress and I hope I don't sound too wistful.

Actually, of course, a night like this is as proud a moment for a wife as it is for her husband.

We know how much our husbands and masters — we might as well pretend, for one night, that they're our masters — look forward to this occasion when they can make up to us for all the nights we stay home alone watching the box.

Our husbands devote a lot of time to Freemasonry and I'm sure I speak for every other wife here when I say that none of us begrudges a moment of the time they spend away from us in the course of their Masonic activities. At least, we know where they are when they're off to the Lodge.

I am not going to say anything about any other activities that might keep some of them away from their wives but what I am going to say is how much we women appreciate this occasion when, on one night a year, we are able to participate.

We know, gentlemen, how valuable we are to you and how you couldn't manage without us, and we know we couldn't manage without you either, though we may not mention it more than once a year.

We are very happy indeed to have been able to tart ourselves up tonight to enjoy with you this wonderful evening.

On behalf of all the women present, may I say thank you for our delightful gifts and, for myself, may I once again express great pride in the fact that I am sitting in this particular seat beside my husband. It is a night neither of us will ever forget.

The way she goes about preparing her own speeches is obviously very instinctive, and she relies a great deal on her antennae to get the atmosphere and feel the vibrations of the moment, to give her her starting point. This is a risky thing to do and requires a lot of nerve, but, of course, marvellous to be able to do. 'If I read a paper to some learned society it sounds inhibited, I sound artificial. So I avoid reading from a paper if possible. I always have an idea of what I am going to say in the back of my mind, and then I assess the audience and plunge in. I do not mind after-dinner speeches because I have time during the meal to assess the audience. I do not like to be the first one to speak, because I like to know the mood of my audience and whether they laugh or not. For instance, not long ago, I had to go to Norwich to address a crowd of insurance people. I thought about it on the way up in the train, and I worked out that there were not many women in the insurance industry, and sure enough they were all men. I was the first speaker. They had all had a good dinner and quite a lot to drink by then, and I knew they did not want to be attacked about women – they were not ready for a Women's Lib deal. So I got the message across in a totally different way. I took the micky out of them. I took my time before I started, I looked at them, and then I began to wonder aloud what their wives were doing while they were dining and drinking, and I wondered, were their wives watching the telly alone, what were they doing while their men were here laughing and talking? Finally, I got them laughing a lot, and then I was able to tell them they were male chauvinist pigs – and I got my message across seriously.' She is able to employ shock tactics. She told me of another time when she was talking to a group of doctors and consultants at Barts. She was talking about her job and talked generally at first, and then wanted to relate it to her audience specifically: 'At the moment I am on the attack when it comes to doctors, they tell women who for some reason or another are in a depressed state – perhaps their marriage has just broken down – they tell them "Pull yourself together". So in the middle of my talk I stopped, and they thought I had dried. I looked down for a moment as if I was thinking what to say next, and then I suddenly looked up and said, "Pull yourselves together!" And it startled them, they looked amazed and started fidgeting. And I said: "that is what you say to people, and that is how they feel." I suppose I try to get a bit of drama into it. I like to sense an audience first, and then say something which immediately arrests their interest.'

Dr Mervyn Stockwood, Bishop of Southwark

We started by talking about different preaching situations, and Dr Stockwood said that the only kind of audience that he found at all difficult was one of diverse age groups. 'If I go to a Church which is celebrating some great festival, everybody turns up – the Scouts and the Cubs and the Guides – and you know quite well that the kids in the Cubs are going to be bored. At the same time I have to speak to the Mayor and the Corporation, so that if you just address the Cubs, the others will think, "Hasn't the Bishop got something to say to us?" So that it is a split audience that I find difficult.'

We then talked about training in speech, and specifically how he learnt. 'In the days when I was preparing we were taught elocution – I remember being taught by Jack Hulbert's father, and he would stand up and read the twentieth chapter of St John. But now of course there are all these audio-visual devices which are all part of the training of the young priest. I had to find my own way through. I think I was lucky, I had the late Rector of Birmingham – Canon Brian Green – who was I suppose one of the great evangelistic preachers of the Church of England of this century, I got to know him when I was a lad and I used to go on missions with him – I think he had about the best preaching delivery I have met. And his way of presenting an address, of getting it over with reason, of always assuming that the person is interested and wants to listen to you, made a great impression on me. I suppose I modelled myself on him a great deal.'

We then got on to the important point of how fully he wrote his sermons. 'I always write my sermons out in full. I would not trust myself to do one extempore for a number of reasons – I find I need the intellectual discipline, otherwise I gas and repeat myself – my mind goes off at a tangent – something interests me. Brevity is such an important thing in preaching. So I normally write everything out in full – even the throw-away remark – and I am a great believer in humour – you can often illustrate your point with a story which is put in an amusing way.'

He went on to say that there were certain themes, such as you have in confirmation services, which were so familiar that he did not necessarily have everything written out. He said he found them particularly exhausting. 'You see it is the only time these kids see a bishop for years, and you have got to try and say something which you hope will register with them. There is a great deal of psychical energy which goes out from you.'

He then went on to describe what it is like to talk in the House of Lords: 'Curiously enough, the place I no longer use a script is the House of Lords, which must be the most difficult place in the world in which to speak – you cannot be intimate there, it is no place for the throw-away remark. There are very few people who can speak well there – Lord Shinwell, he does. The best of all, and I should say there is no one within a hundred miles of him, is Lord Soper. Not only can he speak with such authority, but he can speak on so many subjects, his knowledge is like an encyclopedia, he can switch from the environment with the most detailed accounts of all sorts of things, whether it is the bottom of the sea or mining, to the history of hanging or race segregation, and never a note, and always in the most lovely English.'

As to advice to young clergymen in training, Dr Stockwood had two things to say: 'I heard our present Primate, when he was Archbishop of York, addressing my clergy on giving sermons, and he said, "When I was a young man I thought I should get into one sermon all the creeds and thirty-nine articles – the whole Christian faith. By the time I became principal of a theological college I realized I would have to concentrate on three points, that was as much as anyone could take. By the time I became Bishop of Bradford I realized that that was too much, and it was two points. Now that I am Archbishop of York I realize that it is only one point – and one point only!" So one of the parsons asked him what would happen if he moved to Canterbury – I must remind him of that. That would be one word of advice – make up your mind what to say.'

And the second piece of advice came in this story. 'At my church in Bristol, the curates used to have to send their sermons in to me so that I could read them. And I remember telling them – make up your mind what you want to say, half way through, look at it and say am I saying what I said I would say, and at the end, have I said it. We had a splendid character called Charlie Hodder, whose two places of worship were the church and the pub – he came very regularly to church and he was an excellent person – of the earth earthy – and if one of the curates were not explaining himself in his sermons, I used to write at the bottom: "What does this mean to Charlie Hodder?" Bishop John Robinson, who started his Ministry in my church at Bristol, and is now Dean of Trinity College, Cambridge, still remembers these remarks and says to me: "What does this mean to Charlie Hodder?" '

Richard Baker

From Richard Baker we obviously wanted to know what it was like to work in television, and what the demands were technically. With his very extensive output, apart from reading the news, in writing and taking part in radio programmes, his interest in music and participation in music programmes, and the many narrations he does with orchestras, of pieces like *Peter and the Wolf* and the *Façade suite* which are technically very difficult and exacting, I wondered whether he got vocally tired, and whether he did much in the way of voice exercises, and most important, how he relaxed. This was his answer: 'I always think it is very difficult with the news, because the last half hour before you go on the air is the most tense of the day — you have got the stuff coming at you all the time, there is not a moment when you can totally relax, and very often that goes on until the very second you are on — so the answer is you have got to start the whole process feeling very fresh. I am one of those who can sleep for half an hour or twenty minutes and feel much better for it, and that helps a lot. I do not do much in the way of voice exercises for the news, but I do if I am doing other things like the narrations — *Peter and the Wolf* and *Façade*. *Façade* is the most terrifying test, and I do pick up the exercises I used to do which involve physical relaxation — lying on the floor and relaxing every muscle in turn, or flopping down and letting everything go, and gradually coming up one notch of the spine at a time until you are straight. And then breathing exercises, and then humming and the noises to get your voice forward — and I find them very helpful. I am not very regular about it, though I always mean to be.'

What he said about relaxation was very interesting. 'I find you very often have to make a colossal effort to relax. You have got to make yourself lie down — the first ten minutes are hell, your mind just goes on and on, but then there is another part of you which comes to the surface if you let it. If you consciously make yourself lie still, it evaporates. I think it is all the incidental pressures that are so infuriating — travel delays, interruptions — the unproductive parts of one's life. It is essential to find a way of relaxing.'

I think he is getting at something very interesting when he talks about reading the news, and the fact that you have to be positive and alive, and yet not come between what you are reading and your viewer — and this is a difficult balance to maintain. 'There is an enormous difference in this news-reading business —

it is not great art, but there is a great difference between the performance you give when you are relaxed and the one you give when you are tensed up. You just give the right values to things – you pause the right amount – you convey the sense in an uninterrupted kind of way, and then it has the right sort of urgency – and about once in three weeks I come off thinking I did that rather well – but only about that often!

'If, as you say, I do come over with warmth, I am not aware of it. I think it is the sort of thing that could not happen if one had any sort of barriers. And it is rather a long process you know, I think it probably does take a number of years to become sufficiently relaxed in the medium to get to the point of not being fussed – I do not mean that you do not care.

'I am not aware of putting on any kind of act under any circumstances. There was a time when I read the news when I was slightly aware of having to be authoritative and a bit solemn. I mean it does come at that end of the spectrum, I think it should be done dead straight with no gimmicks or jokes. I think you just do it, but I think at the beginning I was aware of having to be rather more authoritative than I naturally am.

'There is a way of reading the news with comment, but that certainly is not the way that I could do it. It is a straight reading job, I think, and the more you put a false emphasis to it the more irritating it can be. You have got to exist – you cannot not exist – you cannot be totally a mouthpiece – it is an odd little mixture. And perhaps it is a matter of confidence that comes with experience, where you feel able to just sit there and do it without trying to project anything very much – just existing – and perhaps people come to accept you that way. There are other areas where you use other parts of your personality.'

I think what he says there is very interesting, and makes one realize what a very subtle thing this television persona is. About his earlier influences he said this: 'When I left school I was pretty well Cockney and I worked on the "AY's" and the "OH's". The BBC's attitude has changed entirely now towards accent, and I often wonder whether it is the Grammar School influence which is what I came through – the doctrine being one of self-improvement which is not fashionable any more. I am not remotely upper class – my father was a plasterer – and I am not conscious of having tried to become upper class or anything like that, but he was a singer and always spoke extremely well – we all spoke well – he had a thing about speech. I would have hoped my accent was classless.'

Lord Shinwell

As you will imagine, with his vast experience, Lord Shinwell had a lot of splendid advice, very practical and basic, about how to get confidence in yourself. It was also packed with humour.

About his own preparation and style he said: 'First of all I don't prepare speeches, I have not prepared a speech – I use the word prepare with certain reservations – for about forty years. By that I mean I do not write them in advance – except when a Minister with a brief. I find notes an encumbrance; to write a speech would be stilted; it should be fresh.

'I am not a great orator – some people say I am – I am, rather, a debater. To prepare a speech for a debate would be a mistake because one has to adapt oneself to various speeches made in the course of a debate. In the House of Commons they argue, they contend, they bicker, they quarrel. In the Lords we don't do any of these things, that would hardly be expected of us. I occasionally indulge in a bit of rhetoric when in the mood for it, when arguments are presented and I find them imperfect I venture to correct them!

'I have been asked many, many times by younger M.P.s and other people, how is it that I can speak on any subject about which I have some knowledge without a note. So I tell them about my technique.

'I try to get a few clear ideas in my head – maybe three or four points. The ideas must be clear to me – I think about them – and if I can clothe them in the right language I may make a good speech. If the ideas are not as clear as they should be, or if I am not in the mood to join the ideas and the language together, then it is not a good speech. Now sometimes young M.P.s say to me: "I get the ideas, even a lot of ideas, but I cannot express them." I do not accept that. If one has ideas that are clear about a particular topic one ought to be able to express them – one can often do it in conversation, then why not in the course of a speech. I say to them: "You have just been talking your head off for five minutes, why don't you get up and do the same?" They may not like to face an audience – I like a big audience – I always say: "Don't look at them – just you get up and speak." That is what to do, and gradually you get confidence. Just practice.'

What straightforward commonsense. 'It may be desirable for those about to speak to put something down in writing. If they have a typewriter, play about with it, get an idea, try and present it in appropriate language.' He also said something very valuable I think, something which most people overlook, and that is to keep a dictionary to look through to get odd words, always look up unfamiliar words — then you are constantly adding to your vocabulary.

About his own speaking he went on: 'Sometimes I quite deliberately pause and appear to be searching for a word — I may know the word all right but I keep them guessing, then out it comes. It is more interesting that way, and gives them time to follow. It is sometimes said of my speeches that my pauses are more eloquent than my speech, because they are usually accompanied by gesticulation — a bit of drama. One of the difficulties about audiences is that, no matter how intelligent an audience may be, it is difficult to follow a consecutive speech — say over half an hour's duration.

'Sometimes when I am looking down, people think I have got something written, but I have not. I remember an occasion in the House of Commons when I was debating from the front bench, Churchill was opposite, and I was speaking quite eloquently — by which I mean consecutively, not necessarily in language that was superb — and Churchill got up to see what I was doing — I had a sheet of notepaper in front of me with nothing on it. Churchill once said that it was an insult to an audience not to have something prepared — even his repartee was often marked. I have nothing up my sleeve – of course my critics say it is because I cannot read. Not true, I can.'

About his own style, he went on: 'What is very important is to have a sense of humour, to be able to deploy it — I find I can do this. To give you an example; during the last election I was at a meeting in Crawley — a huge audience — I looked at the audience and said: "Have you ever heard of Napoleon Bonaparte?", they were all astonished — a remarkable opening gambit — I said: "You must have heard of him, the Emperor of France, well of course you have heard of him." I said: "You know what he did — he vanquished the Spaniards and he destroyed the Dutch, and then he thought he'd have a go at Russia, but the weather was bad, so he returned. Then he declared: 'I am going to make of England an off-shore island of France' — that is actually what he said — you can challenge me, but go and read it." I added: "But he failed — you know he failed — now it is left for Mr Heath to do it." They roared with laughter; after that I could have said anything.' It is impossible here to indicate the inflection and timing of that — you must imagine it. And he went on: 'Another time, there was a lot of talk about the miners — I started off the meeting: "I see the miners want more money" — well it was dealing with the subject – I said: "Anybody here doesn't want more money?" And an extraordinary thing happened, one man put up his hand and everybody laughed. One must be able to do that kind of thing, it is required if one is to capture the attention of an audience.'

He summed it all up in a marvellous way: 'Getting clear ideas is very important. In fact I would go so far as to say that nobody has a right to address a public meeting unless his ideas on a particular subject are worth hearing. Also, many ideas are picked up in the course of conversation and can be employed when addressing an audience. Then there is the matter of enunciation – mine is very good I believe – Lord Hailsham, by no means a special friend of mine, referred to my timing one day after I had spoken. You have to time it – no need to rush – one should speak carefully, quietly timing it, this is essential – and then say something with passion which indicates sincerity – how one really feels about the subject.

In fact I would go so far as to say that one never ought to speak at all unless you have the sincerity which justifies appearing in front of an audience. You either believe what you say or you don't believe, then it is possible to convey sincerity.'

This last paragraph sums it all up – what you believe is your *raison d'être* – your reason for being there.

These were the views of some of the prominent speakers with whom I talked when I wrote this book twenty years ago. Much of what they said is as relevant now as it was then and is both illuminating and helpful, but fashions and needs change, so I felt it was important to talk to some people who are in the public eye and ear now. As well as the questions I asked before about nerves, how you prepare, and so on, I wanted to find out:

i. how much they feel the media has changed the way people speak in public, and how media reportage influences or affects them personally;

ii. how they thought accents were perceived now, and to what extent we were still influenced by old standards;

iii. whether they felt that styles of speaking have become more forceful: has an element of bullying replaced the democracy of argument?

iv. how much were they aware of the form and rhetorical shape of a speech when they were preparing one;

v. do people speak as well as they used to, and to what extent have marketing ploys affected this?

vi. do people still enjoy hearing good public speaking?

Now I believe the answer to the last question is categorically yes: and as you will see, each of the speakers I talked to expressed the same belief.

There is a great need for words after all: if you go to a funeral, for instance, you are moved by the words said, whether you believe in religion or not – they help to assuage and lay to rest. Alternatively, if we listen to a good comic, the form and rhythms (what we call timing) make us laugh as much as what is said. And then one thinks back to nursery rhymes and the joy involved in that last rhyme.

In 1986 I took part in one of Granada's 'World in Action' programmes. It focused on a very interesting book called *Our Master's Voices* by Max Atkinson (published by Methuen). In it Atkinson analysed the techniques of successful speech-making. Perhaps you start with a question or a riddle to get people interested; then you begin to argue that question through. You build examples up in threes, and on the way you use a certain amount of alliteration and assonance (all techniques of rhetoric that Shakespeare used so wonderfully) and you end with the conclusion to the argument. (This is just a very brief summary of Atkinson's analysis, and of course you need to read the whole of his book to understand it fully.)

The Granada programme involved a new SDP candidate, Ann Brennan, who was to take part in the Party's annual conference in Buxton: with a number of other new candidates, she was given four minutes to speak. Ann Brennan gave Max Atkinson the gist of her speech, he put it into a form which accorded to his theory, and I coached her in the speaking of it. The experiment was so successful, with people on their feet applauding, that in fact she only got through half her speech in the allotted time. Of course the content was good, but more important, the form of the speech was just right – such was the power of the form.

For the new edition of this book I talked to Neil Kinnock, Helena Kennedy and Tariq Ali, who all generously responded and gave their time. I particularly wanted to talk to them because each one has a deep belief in the need for debate, and cares about people being able to express their views. Each one also happens to be an excellent public speaker with power and charisma, and each comes from a very different perspective.

In my introduction I said that you will only feel truly confident if you feel true to yourself, and each of these speakers in different words said precisely the same thing – that you need to be rooted in what you are saying. They also felt that there was a genuine hunger for debate.

Each of the three obviously had things to say about nerves and how to deal with them. They were also interesting about accents: on the whole it was felt that there was now a much greater acceptance of accents, and that the voice of authority was no longer necessarily linked to a Received Pronunciation – though as you will see there was some ambivalence about this, which I think reflects the complexity of the issue now. They were all very aware of form in a speech – i.e. the need to grab attention at the beginning, to build through argument and to conclude that argument with some kind of flourish, perhaps with a surprising word or with humour. They were each quite objective about themselves and very aware of the need for style and shape.

But I suppose the question that brought the most interesting and vigorous responses was the one about the media and media reportage, and how that has changed the whole perception of speaking in public. Unanimously they felt that because reporting has become so partial it acts as a kind of unofficial dictatorship: now many speakers feel that everything has to be written down for fear that a spontaneous comment, on the spur of the moment, may give the wrong nuance, and will be misinterpreted. And they all agreed, sadly, that the age of the speech-writer is here.

Because these issues of the media, the perception of accents and the form of a speech are now so interlinked, their answers did not run in any particular order but ranged around the subject as a whole. And I have tried to report them like that, because I think the way they talked gives us an insight into them as people – and into their warmth and humour.

Neil Kinnock

I began by asking him how the approach to speaking has changed in the last twenty years: he felt that the main difference was 'in the ease and frequency with which everyone now uses microphones: even fifteen years ago there was no guarantee that even quite a large meeting would have the facilities of loudspeaker equipment. The fact that in the last ten years it is unusual not to have access to a microphone means that you can speak much more easily, and be fairly confident that the audience is going to hear you – and you can also use nuance'. So the microphone takes away some of the strain on the voice and allows us to catch a more intimate tone if need be.

I next asked him how much he was aware of the shaping of a speech and whether the presence of microphones made any difference to that: 'To me, no. Even before I wrote speeches – and that is the great change, I now write speeches – even before that, I always used to have a structure. A speech is a sort of participatory lesson – you try to impart some new knowledge, some new enlightenment – and perhaps a couple of new jokes.' He went on: 'The bits of speeches that people tend to remember, that appear in a dictionary of quotations, are almost always the bits which I have used unrehearsed and unwritten. They are the lines which come from the base of my spine as I speak them.' He then explained why he now writes speeches: 'Whilst I was leader of the Party I could be absolutely certain that any sentence that didn't have the correct syntax or had a colourful reference that came as I spoke would be the one thing that would be picked up and hurled back at me.'

I then wanted to know if he felt people had become more forceful in the way they spoke in public – that because of the need to coin the soundbite, etc., they were not investigating thoughts, perhaps because they felt the need to be more combative. His answer: 'What I note is that there is much less use of dark and light in speaking – people are not communicating with the audience in the room – they are talking to the microphone, to the radio, to the television camera.' And this I think was the nub of his argument: 'All the people in the room are there for the whole of the speech, whereas by definition all the reports of that speech will be partial. And so we have a kind of dictatorship – the dictatorship which will use a phrase that is particularly graphic or could be potentially embarrassing: some will play up to that particular gallery, but others are forced into being straightjacketed – and end up being extremely boring.' He went on to say, 'Since we face a completely electronic future, I don't think we will ever rid ourselves now of the fear of misreporting and misinterpretation.'

And so, of course, we got on to the role of the speech-writer – interesting because it is a relatively new departure and one which I feel carries many implications. He said: 'The age of the speech-writer has arrived, and because they don't make speeches themselves their purpose is to pack into a written speech as much information as they think is necessary – plus a few good lines.' He went on to say that this did not take into account the different mood and feelings of each particular audience, and also, because they were not your own words, the speech called for some kind of acting in putting it over – he would feel totally false doing it. He recounted with regret that he could never use speeches written for him: 'My life would have been easier and my time more plentiful if I'd felt comfortable using other people's words.'

Regarding his background: 'My father was a strong, nearly silent man – a lovely man – who would occasionally come out with wise sayings that came from deep down in the pit – not the coal mine you understand!' And he laughed and added, 'Perhaps it does come from there.' He remembers that if someone said they could not understand why 'someone so intelligent had done something foolish', his father would say, 'There is no shortage of intelligence – it is bloody common sense there is a shortage of.' His mother was an extremely cogent woman, coherent in argument – but neither had ever spoken in public. Yet immediately I had the impression of a family that valued words.

Asked about nerves: 'I do get nervous – in a sense a degree of nervousness is essential, but I always want to establish a relationship with an audience – I feel my way a little in order to see where the pulse is.'

What he said about accents was most interesting: by putting it into an historical context, he reflected just how much fashions in speech change: 'Because of the way the voices of authority in advertising and newscasting have a particular kind of accent, an expectation has been created that voices of authority in politics should have much the same accent.' He felt that eighty years ago even establishment politicians would often have slightly regional accents. Later the conformity of authoritative accents came in, interspersed with people with strong provincial accents, who became a source of strength: 'Now we have moved to the era of advertising and newscasting, it is not as easy to get yourself listened to for what you are saying. It certainly had an effect on how I was reported and regarded – but that is also true of John Major, who is subject to certain mispronunciations. For the verbal cartoonist, it's a gift. I am much easier to impersonate than to draw. But does anyone remember Attlee being impersonated – or Nye Bevan?'

Lastly, in answer to the question of whether we have become a less verbal society, he said: 'As a 52-year-old with relatively conservative taste and radical politics, it does seem to me we hear more talking but what we also hear is the continual repetition of catchphrases drawn from the American idiom or from advertising. There is more talk but I am not sure whether there is more listening, and there is less effective verbal communication: the massive extension in the use of euphemism makes language bland. However, when people encounter well-constructed and meaningful speech, particularly in good theatre or good film, then they cherish it.'

Advice: 'You must be engaged in politics to try to serve people: if that is your purpose then whatever the place of communication, whether you are talking in the intimacy of the Saturday morning surgery or addressing a crowd in Trafalgar Square, the emphasis must be on imparting something to them – and being interested in their view. You have got to seek to communicate.' He remembers the advice of an old friend, Bill Gregory, whom he knew when he started in adult education: a remarkable man, an educator and agitator all his life, Gregory said, 'Always aim a little above their heads because they will reach up: if you aim at their bellies, they will think with their balls.' In other words, talk to people's intelligence.

I was personally very gratified to hear him say: 'In the wake of my losing my voice in 1983, which occurred as a result of making ninety-odd speeches in the three weeks of the General Election campaign, mostly out of doors or in smoky halls without the use of a microphone, the one piece of advice I really took was Cic Berry's – "Speak with your feet flat on the ground".' He said that was the best practical advice he had ever had!

In a postscript he sent me after the interview he wrote: 'One thing that is worth saying is that today's "soundbite" is, in some ways, the equivalent of yesterday's great and memorable statement – see Churchill, Lincoln, Bevan, Napoleon – et al!'

My feeling was that this is a man with a profound sense of what he wants to say, and a joy in communicating it to other people, not for his own sense of importance, but rather because he genuinely wants those ideas understood. And furthermore, with a conviction that we must be aware of the media, but use it for good: and that, most important, people enjoy communicating.

Helena Kennedy

Here was a very different perspective from Neil Kinnock's: a Queen's Counsel rather than a Member of Parliament; a woman's view in a man's world; and a woman with a strong Scottish accent to boot.

I started with the media, asking the same questions as before. Her answer: 'I certainly think there has been an incredible shift: when I started we were hearing the news and listening to people communicating about the serious things in life and they were speaking in the received BBC voice: I think that now there is an acceptance that the media is in many ways the camp-fire around which our communities gather, and therefore if it is going to have any validity at all it has to have the voices of us all. It is important for people to hear themselves in the voices that are communicating to them about the world's events, or about social problems – for too long it was only the voice of the upper middle class who could speak with weight and gravitas. It has been an important part of the democratization of our world that we are hearing the voices of other people: there has been a shift in power – probably not enough – but at least a shift is taking place. And I see myself as one of the people who are an example of that shift.' She went on: 'One of the advantages I have always felt was that I didn't speak in the way that most barristers spoke. I not only had the advantage of being different, it also meant that there was an immediacy, particularly with people on juries and with my clients, which I think they found welcome.'

My next question was about any influences on her when she was young, although neither parent did any public speaking. 'My father, albeit a Glaswegian working-class man, had a particularly nice voice – people would remark on it. I liked verse at school – I liked hearing it – and I have always been very interested in the spoken word. I enjoyed public speaking and liked to debate.' This last obviously increased with her interest in politics.

I asked if she ever felt nervous: 'If the ideas are strong, I have no problem with nerves – the need to get the ideas across and to persuade the court, or the judge if I am mitigating for a client. I find it more difficult and am more inclined to be nervous when I am dealing with technical matters rather than the substance of someone's life.'

I saw there was a difference here between dealing with something which was within the range of one's job, and perhaps making a formal speech, so I asked her about this: 'Doing my job has never been a problem – but when I was first asked to make an after-dinner speech I was very nervous. But I actually now love it – I have cracked it! Part of this is about gender.' This was just what I wanted her to get on to. 'Why women find after-dinner speaking so hard is that on the whole women don't like telling jokes. I don't ever do a string of jokes. I always find something important that I want to be saying: I find the heart of the message – and one should be building towards that as a serious finale – but there has to be humour and warmth in it. You must weave humour into the message.'

Are you conscious of the shape of a speech? 'I am conscious of a shape – I am the same when I am making a speech to the jury. Even in cross-examination I am conscious of having signposts – I have a journey that I want to take a witness on, a place where I want to get them, but you have to be flexible enough to respond to their answers; the failed cross-examination is when you don't listen to the answer.'

She went further: 'In a speech to the jury you have to engage their interest, so in the beginning you have to somehow make the issue crystallize, and you have to find some sort of peg that helps you to carry it – some sort of analogy. I am a great believer that the law need not be as obscure and covered in mystification as it is. I think the real challenge to lawyers is to make the law simple, so if you can use imagery but use simple language it's wonderful. And to use language occasionally that slightly shocks the form that you are in – not enough to seem disrespectful or take away from the dignity of the process, but to use language that surprises – because the formality can make everything so bland.'

To illustrate her point she went on: 'I remember lawyers laughing – I was talking about police officers embellishing evidence, and of course I didn't want to suggest that they were lying, so I said "You can understand why someone might be tempted to dolly up the evidence".' 'Dolly' was the word that surprised here – just as the analogy of 'the camp-fire' had grabbed me when we first started to talk.

She continued: 'Just as in the theatre styles have changed – the grand style of Kean would now be too overblown – in the same way advocacy has changed; some of that Marshall Hall style, or Sir Patrick Hastings, would be just over the top now and unacceptable. The media has made a lot of difference.'

As a woman, how difficult was it for you at the beginning to gain respect? 'It is harder for a woman to be an authoritative figure or voice. And there is no doubt I had to fight harder for my place – not to be the little girl – and I had to find a way of doing it without being tight-lipped or humourless: it was quite hard when one was young. I tried to turn it on its head by making my skill about being real – not by being middle-class, public school and male, but by making it seem that their way was inappropriate and mine was the right way.'

How much are we caught up in the soundbite, and are we exploring thought? 'That is one of the things that concerns me most about what is happening to politics – and why it is so hard to get at the truth. Time is the constraint; nobody ever has proper debate, proper exploration. And a very prevalent feeling here in Britain is that ideas are somehow in bad form. There is a way in which we don't engage with ideas, and that is terrible: it undermines democracy, because without knowledge how can we make real decisions? Knowledge comes from communication.'

Do you think people still enjoy hearing good speaking? 'I do. I chair Charter 88, which is about seeking a bill of rights and wanting more accountability in government – and we have been having a series of lectures, and it is amazing how many people turn up.'

Have you been helped by any good advice? 'I remember a senior woman at the Bar, who was a great friend, talking to me about fear. She said, "We are all much the same – when you are in front of those three Appeal Court judges, just imagine them naked, sitting in the bath."'

What advice have you to give? 'Don't try to be like anybody else. Find your own way of doing it, that you feel comfortable with: watch other people, not because you want to be like them, but so you can draw on their experience. Map something out – have a plan – and keep it simple.' Her last words were: 'Women do not use the grand style: recognize that speaking is about communication and not about performing, and if you do the communication well, the performance will follow. I also know that when you are speaking to the jury, if you do it like a man the men don't like you – and neither do the women.'

Here was someone not only with a belief in her work and what she had to do, but with a belief in other people and their need to communicate: and this put it all in perspective. Added to which, she has a great and vivid sense of humour.

'Don't try to be like anybody else – find your own way of doing it': that seems to me the message we should take with us.

Tariq Ali

As with the others I began by asking how much he thought the media had changed the way we speak in public. 'I think the media has affected people in the last ten years in particular because television and the television news, with some exceptions, tends to go for the soundbite, so lots of politicians have forgotten the art of public speaking and go for what they think is a clever or a pithy phrase which will get on the six o'clock news – and I think this has been a disaster: if you switch on the radio when they are broadcasting the House of Commons you will hear very few good speeches these days. The last really powerful speech in the Commons was Geoffrey Howe's resignation speech which was wonderful: it was effective, it was dramatic, the cadences were wonderful, people were waiting for every single sentence to finish. But that is very rare – and that of course is a speech which brought Mrs Thatcher down, a speech which toppled a Prime Minister, showing the importance of the spoken word as it is heard by millions on radio and television. By and large it is the desire to be clever without too much substance – so lots of politicians go to speech-writers, who come up with a clever sentence, and the whole structure of the speech, which should have a beginning, a middle, and an end, has gone. During the last election campaigns one noticed this – politicians were repetitive, they were waffling, they were incoherent – very few came up to scratch.'

He went on: 'The other problem – that even in the election campaigns of the sixties and seventies, the political leaders like Heath and Wilson had to speak at public meetings. Public meetings were not controlled as they are now: nowadays by and large they rely on radio and television or they have special public meetings where TV cameras are present and only the faithful are allowed to attend, and they are told – "the cameras are here so behave yourselves". In other words, something that used to be the lifeblood of election campaigning – a real live audience with hecklers – has gone, and so there is nothing to stimulate the speaker. Also they depend on PR outfits – one reason why politics is in such a bad state is that people are not taken in by politicians groomed by media specialists, who get paid millions for it.'

Although he doesn't do a great deal of public speaking any more, I asked him how much he had enjoyed it at the height of the radical movement in the sixties and seventies, when he spoke to as many as fifteen meetings a week. 'You learnt the art of public speaking on your feet, and I enjoyed it enormously. The only thing which got on my nerves was hearing myself repeat myself – something you have to do when you are speaking in different places. I used to vary it as much as possible. I think a live audience is crucial: often you pick up vibes from an audience, and sometimes you can be thrown by one person – who may perhaps have a nervous smile, and you think that perhaps you are not being convincing – and at the end when you go and talk to them you find that they had really enjoyed it. I love speaking to live audiences because of the feedback which keeps you going.'

How objective are you, and how conscious of shaping a speech? 'I don't think I have ever written a speech from A to Z, but I make notes, and I work my way through them: often I used to change course in the middle of a speech, I would shape it while I was going along. It was the ending peroration which gave one the most problems because I hated ending the speech the same way – and that's the one thing I never did. So even if the arguments were the same, I used to find different ways of ending them.'

What was your family influence? 'My father was a great public speaker: he was President of the All India Students' Federation in the late thirties and he won all sorts of prizes. And while I was in Pakistan I was quite an active debater. It was at a time when there was a military dictatorship there, so you couldn't just blurt stuff out: everything had to be carefully worked so that when you spoke people were forced to derive meanings from your words – the meanings were there but they were hidden meanings. So when I used to speak I learnt how to choose words carefully – a very major thing.'

About nerves: 'Yes, before a big speech I am always a bit nervous. A few months ago I went to the Oxford Union, and as I hadn't spoken publicly for a long time, I was nervous. But it was a warm audience, and the tricks of the trade soon came back.'

Do you think we are no longer a verbal society? 'One of the things which happened in the eighties was a real regression in terms of a critical culture – the art of criticism has been replaced by hype and point-scoring, and this has also affected public speaking. The content has disappeared: it is the form which has obsessed people – how do I look, how does it sound – and not what it is that you are saying.'

Did you have any advice when you started that you could pass on?

'No. I just learnt it on the trot. What is crucial is that you do your own research. So many politicians rely on researchers, it is obvious these days when you hear them talking that they haven't mastered their brief. In some cases, when you know a researcher is very intelligent, you can hear the researcher's words being spoken through a puppet, but the puppet doesn't understand it – it's quite sad!' He went on: 'A key element of being a good public speaker is that you believe in what you are saying: a belief in yourself and a belief in something.'

Finally, we got on to the subject of theatre, and he told me a great story. He wrote a play with Howard Brenton called *Moscow Gold* which was put on at the Barbican Theatre by the RSC: the play was about Gorbachev. They took some scenes from the play to Moscow, and after the performance a leading Soviet actress came up to David Calder, who was playing Gorbachev, and hugged him, and said that even though she couldn't understand the language, she was just very moved by hearing how he said the words and the look in his eyes – and for the first time she said she felt sympathetic to 'our leader'. I think this story illustrates the power of live communication, which to me is something we have to fight for and keep alive.

Talking to him, one was aware of someone who was very clear about what needed to be said, and who was wonderfully articulate. But there was something more: the care with which he chose his words – perhaps because English is not his only language, and perhaps because he knows that words can be dangerous – made it a great pleasure to listen to him. His advice, 'Believe in what you are saying, and believe in yourself', seemed to me the key to what he said.

There is a great deal of wisdom that can be gleaned from what has been said. Each of the speakers obviously has an instinctive knowledge of how to communicate with an audience, each one is able to use language creatively, each one knows how to engage an audience. What you have to do is employ these pointers in your own way – it is often necessary to model yourself on someone while your own style emerges – but finally what you say and how you say it has to be completely your own.

In any case, some will want to take it further than others. And should you want to study more, then get hold of books of speeches and read them, and get to know their rhythm and style and how it is possible to build a speech. But for most people, I think, what has been said is enough.

Finally, remember, an exchange takes place between you and your listeners, and you need to be as open to them as you wish them to be receptive to you.

On the following pages are details of other books by Cicely Berry and available from Virgin

VOICE AND THE ACTOR

'Technique as such is a myth, for there is no such thing as a correct voice. There is no right way – there are only a million wrong ways.'

Voice and the Actor is the first classic work by Cicely Berry, Voice Director of the Royal Shakespeare Company and world famous voice teacher. Encapsulating her renowned method of teaching voice production, the exercises in this straightforward, no-nonsense guide will develop relaxation, breathing and muscular control – without which no actor or speaker can achieve their full potential.

Voice and the Actor is the essential first step towards speaking a text with truth and meaning. Inspiring and practical, her words will be a revelation for beginner and professional alike.

'Cicely Berry would never try to separate the sound of words from their living context. For her the two are inseparable. This is what makes her book so necessary and valuable.'

– from the foreword by Peter Brook

ISBN 0 245 52021 X

THE ACTOR AND THE TEXT

'Without Cicely Berry, without her talent, my journey from film back to Shakespeare would have been impossible. *The Actor and the Text* . . . is the essential key to opening up the secrets of a difficult text to a wider audience.'

– Jeremy Irons

The Actor and the Text – now in a new and expanded edition – is Cicely Berry's classic book, distilled from years of working with actors of the highest calibre.

Building on the specific exercises covered in her first book, *Voice and the Actor*, she relates the practicality of voice production to the challenges of a difficult text. And by getting inside the words we use – whether those of Shakespeare or our contemporaries – she shows how to release their energy and excitement for an audience.

'*The Actor and the Text* will be used by actors and directors of every kind – amateur, professional, occasional and obsessional.'

– from the foreword by Trevor Nunn

ISBN 0 86369 705 4